More Than
Just BS

More Than Just BS

Sly tips on BS/MD, combined & accelerated medical program admissions – from a student who got in

Jayson Marwaha

To order additional copies of this book, contact:
Xlibris Corporation
1-888-795-4274
www.Xlibris.com
Orders@Xlibris.com
123159

Short Table of Contents

Introduction 11
Chapter 1: Guaranteed medical *what?*: The low-down on GMed programs........13

UNIT I: The Preparation Plan: Building your resume and
demonstrating your passion for medicine 21

Chapter 2: What to do while you're in middle school...............................26
Chapter 3: What to do while you're in 9th grade...32
Chapter 4: What to do while you're in 10th grade 42
Chapter 5: What to do while you're in 11th grade 47
Chapter 6: What to do while you're in 12th grade 61

UNIT II: The Application Process...67

Chapter 7: Overview and timeline: What to expect from GMed apps...................70
Chapter 8: What happens after you submit your application,
        and how the review process works..76
Chapter 9: Where to apply: Putting the final tweaks on your list of schools........80
Chapter 10: Where do I start?!?: How to handle all the work.............................85
Chapter 11: The written application..90
Chapter 12: Interviews..121
Chapter 13: Making a decision..140

APPENDIX: List of all GMed programs in the US..143
About the Author 165

Real Table of Contents

Introduction 11
    Why you just bought this book... 11

Chapter 1: Guaranteed medical *what?:*
    The low-down on GMed programs.. 13
    The basics 13
    Things that all GMed programs have in common............................. 15
    A bit more on the accelerated medical program.............................. 16
    Some questions you probably have by now
        (and my attempt at answering them for you) 17
    How to use the rest of this book 19

UNIT I: The Preparation Plan: Building your resume
and demonstrating your passion for medicine 21

Introduction to the next few years of your life.................................... 23

Chapter 2: What to do while you're in middle school............................ 26
    Middle school classes and grades 27
    Extracurriculars 27
    Looking ahead to high school... 28
    Summary and checklist... 31

Chapter 3: What to do while you're in 9th grade.................................... 32
    Academics 33
    Keeping an eye on standardized tests 34
    Clubs, activities, and general resume-building.................................. 35
    Taking it all back to our master resume template 37
    Summary and checklist... 40

Chapter 4: What to do while you're in 10th grade 42
    Academics 43
    Clubs, activities, and general resume-building.................................. 43
    Summer after 10th grade 45
    Summary and checklist... 46

Chapter 5: What to do while you're in 11th grade 47
   Academics 47
   Standardized tests...49
   Clubs, activities, and general resume-building......................52
   Deciding where to apply..54
   Summer after 11th grade 55
   Summary and checklist...59

Chapter 6: What to do while you're in 12th grade 61
   Academics 62
   Standardized tests...62
   Clubs, activities, and general resume-building......................63
   Summary and checklist...65

UNIT II: The Application Process...67

Introduction 69

Chapter 7: Overview and timeline: What to expect from GMed apps...................70
   Application components..71
   Timeline 73
   Summary...74

Chapter 8: What happens after you submit your application, and
      how the review process works 76
   The review process 77
   Summary...79

Chapter 9: Where to apply: Putting the final tweaks
      on your list of schools..80
   A quick recap from Chapter 5: Coming up with
     a preliminary list of schools..80
   Safety checks: Making sure your list of schools is *smart*...........81
   Some advice for the rest of you...83
   Conclusion 84
   Summary...84

Chapter 10: Where do I start?!?: How to handle all the work..................85
   Your 3-step, kick-app strategy...86
   Conclusion 88
   Summary...89

Chapter 11: The written application 90
    Letters of recommendation 91
    The resume: Putting it all together 95
    The essays 103
    Everything else on the written application 116

Chapter 12: Interviews 121
    Alumni interviews 122
    GMed interviews 129

Chapter 13: Making a decision 140
    Summary 142

APPENDIX: List of all GMed programs in the US 143
About the Author 165

INTRODUCTION

Why you just bought this book

L OG ON TO Facebook to gossip, stalk, or a little bit of both, and you'll inevitably see one or two sidebar advertisements offering to "chance" you for Harvard, Princeton, or Stanford. Open the "Spam" folder in your inbox and you'll find promotional e-mails from colleges you never knew existed. Dust the cobwebs off of your library card and visit your local library (ha – I bet you haven't done *that* in a while) and you'll see shelves upon shelves of books claiming to help you *Crack! Crush! Dominate! Ace!*, or if they think they're too cool, *Pwn!* the college admissions process. Pretty much every Joe Blow has offered up his two cents on college apps on the internet. Face it: info on the undergraduate admissions process is not just easy to find – you're practically drowning in it.

But what about guaranteed medical programs?

First of all, if you have no idea what I'm talking about, no worries – I'll fill you in. If you've read this far and you're not bored yet, you're probably either 1) a high school student who knows he/she wants to study and practice medicine in the future, or 2) the parent of such a child (or, you could just be doing a little light reading . . . I guess that's cool, too).

You might've heard some rumors already – med school apps are killers, guaranteed medical program apps are nightmares – and they've scared you straight. So you went to a bookstore and saw *nothing* on guaranteed medical programs (hereafter referred to as GMed programs). Then, you looked them up online and found that there are no more than three or four books in existence on the subject. Problem is, half of them were written by people who never went through the GMed application process themselves, and the other half are filled with tons of unnecessary info that you don't really need to hear.

That's where this book comes in. The application process for GMed programs *is* a deadeningly monotonous, overwhelmingly demanding, and tremendously stressful experience – if you jump in unprepared. But with the right advice from the right guy, you don't have to feel like you're being pecked to death by ducks while you're filling out your apps.

I've made this book completely BS-free. There are no fancy quotes from famous dead people, no lousy jokes – *just solid, proven tips on how to guarantee yourself a seat in med school and a future in medicine.* This book has a detailed prep plan and checklist that tells you everything you need to do between middle school and the end of your senior year to be prepared. It also has detailed sections devoted entirely to making sure your apps are compelling, but don't take you eons to complete. In this book, I obsessively overanalyze every step of the application process so unbelievably close that I almost considered seeing a psychiatrist when I was done.

You can take comfort in knowing that these are all tips that I developed and used to get into some of the nation's top 6-, 7-, and 8-year GMed programs including the ones at Brown University, Caltech and the UC San Diego School of Medicine, and Penn State and Jefferson Medical College, to name a few.

With this book, you'll be prepared for every crazy essay prompt, cranky interviewer, and competitive applicant resume that GMed programs could ever throw at you. So what are you waiting for? Let's do this.

CHAPTER 1

Guaranteed medical *what?:*
The low-down on GMed programs

Y OU KNOW HOW airplane crews
always roll down the ceiling
television sets before takeoff to show you those super-boring safety videos? You can
always tell when someone's never flown before because they're anxiously craning
their neck trying to memorize every word of the subtitles. Meanwhile, everyone
else is staring out the window thinking, "You shouldn't need a freakin' video to
figure out how to put on a seat belt. And where the hell are my free peanuts?!" Well,
the GMed version of that video is about to begin now. For those of you who have
no idea what a GMed program is, prepare to crane your neck forward. For the rest
of you, calm down . . . peanuts will be served shortly.

The basics

First of all, you should know that these programs have about a hundred
different names, but all refer to the same concept of a program that guarantees med
school acceptance to high school seniors. Some of the most common names I've
seen include: BA/MD program, BS/MD program, accelerated medical program,
combined medical program, direct medical program, and of course, guaranteed
medical program. For the purposes of sounding way cooler than everyone else,
we'll be referring to them as GMed programs.

Before I explain to you the concepts behind GMed programs, it's important that you first understand the standard route taken by the vast majority of students in the US to earn their MD degree and practice medicine. Here's how that process normally goes:

Step 1 (4 years): Little Johnny is a high school student who has absolutely no idea what he wants to do with the rest of his life. Little Johnny drifts blissfully through high school and does reasonably well in his classes.

Step 2 (4 years): Little Johnny is now an undergraduate student. In his sophomore year, he realizes that medicine is the field for him – he now knows that he wants to be a doctor when he grows up. Little Johnny frantically begins preparing for the MCAT (quite possibly the cruelest exam in the world) and spends the rest of his sophomore, junior, and senior years gearing his classes, thoughts, and activities toward med school. After three years of hardship and inestimable sleepless nights competing with fellow students for grades, resume-building opportunities, and better-looking med school applications, Little Johnny is robbed of all his childhood innocence. Luckily, he just barely manages to get into a med school in the US.

Step 3 (4 years): Now that he's in med school, a now tired, overworked, and caffeine-addicted Lil J must decide upon a specialty that he wishes to pursue (some examples include: internal medicine, radiology, gastroenterology, and surgery). Lil J now applies for the residency of his choice. (In case you're wondering, he changed his name to Lil J because he records and sells underground rap records to pay for med school.)

Step 4 (number of years depends on one's specialty): Johnny residencies and fellowships himself into oblivion until, moments before burnout, he can finally practice medicine on his own.

That's the process that most people go through. Okay fine, it's generally not *that* brutal . . . but it's still pretty long and pretty taxing. It's important to know that the transition from step 2 to step 3 – applying to med school – is unbelievably competitive, stressful, and uncertain. The application process is incredibly hard, and the majority of students dying to study medicine aren't offered a position in *any* med school in the US. According to the Association of American Medical Colleges, for the 2009-2010 entering class, the national med school acceptance rate was 43.5% – that is, of the 42,269 students applying to med school, only 18,390 got into at least one. That means the remaining 56.5% didn't get into a single med school and were left with *three* options:

1) Pursue a career in something else,
2) Apply to med school again the following year, or
3) Go to a foreign med school (which I don't recommend due to the additional level of bureaucracy the US places on people with foreign medical degrees).
4) Oops ... I almost forgot a fourth option: Learn to look like you really care when you ask the question, "Do you want fries with that?"

The GMed program was primarily created to ensure that you don't have to worry about the possibility of being shut out by medical schools; it virtually eliminates the med school application process for undergraduate students by "guaranteeing" high school graduates a seat in med school once they complete their undergraduate degree. The catch is, as a high school student, you have to have already made up your mind that medicine is the right profession for you.

High school seniors apply to these programs during the regular undergraduate application process. If they are offered admission to a GMed program, they are accepted to the undergraduate school and are also "guaranteed" acceptance to the affiliated med school after obtaining a bachelor's degree. The undergraduate school and med school components of GMed programs are often part of the same university (such as Brown University and Brown Medical School), but don't always have to be (such as Caltech and UC San Diego School of Medicine).

Things that all GMed programs have in common

There are a couple of basic things shared by all GMed programs that you should be aware of:

1) They are incredibly hard to get into. The more popular GMed programs receive a couple thousand applications every year, and almost never more than 50 – usually around 30 – students are accepted (some accept as many as 100, some as low as 6). That's about a 2-5% acceptance rate window. Also, most GMed applications are noticeably harder and lengthier than regular undergraduate applications, and with good reason: you're practically applying to an undergraduate school and a med school at the same time.

2) Once you get in, they ease up on you a bit. GMed programs don't exactly offer "guaranteed" med school acceptance – rather, it's more like "conditional" or "provisional" acceptance because there are certain requirements you have to fulfill as an undergraduate student to keep your guaranteed med school seat, such as maintaining a certain GPA and taking some required science classes. However, achieving these requirements is

literally a cakewalk compared to the standard med school application process. Some common requirements and guidelines include:\

a. Maintaining a GPA of at least 3.0 or 3.5 (the minimum acceptable GPA varies between programs)
b. Taking most or all of the classes included in the standard pre-med curriculum
c. No MCAT! That's right: many GMed programs eliminate the need to take the MCAT (the evil medical equivalent of the SAT that normal undergraduate students take). Some GMed programs *do* require you to take the exam, but they have reasonably low MCAT score baselines that you must exceed in order to preserve your acceptance to med school. Either way, it's less stressful and much easier than actually applying to med school.
d. Many GMed programs give you the freedom to major in anything you want – anything from anthropology to religious studies – as long as you take those pre-med courses mentioned above. Other GMed programs require you to major in something science-related.

The two different types of GMed programs

Remember how Little Johnny spent four years as an undergraduate student? Some GMed programs allow you to shorten that by one or two years so you can get your MD degree a bit sooner. Thus, there are two types of GMed programs:

1) Accelerated GMed programs (2 or 3 undergraduate years + 4 med school years = 6 or 7 total years until you get your MD)
2) Normal-pace GMed programs (4 undergraduate years + 4 med school years = 8 total years until you get your MD)

A bit more on the accelerated medical program

The philosophy behind the accelerated program is that, if you're a high school graduate and you're already certain that you want to study medicine, then you don't need to spend a full four years as an undergraduate student discovering your interests and taking unnecessary classes. You should just move on to med school as fast as possible. As such, 6 – and 7-year accelerated programs usually squeeze the standard undergraduate pre-med curriculum into 2 or 3 years, so you learn all the same foundational science in less time. At the end of your second or third year as an undergraduate, you'll be given your (most likely science-related) bachelor's degree. Some accelerated programs will let you finish up your bachelor's degree while you're in your first year of med school, so you could be working towards two degrees at the same time. But that's complicated – let's worry about getting *in* first.

The concept of the accelerated GMed program is a very contentious one, primarily because of the following two questions that critics and naysayers usually bring up:

Don't 6 – and 7-year programs make you less prepared to be a doctor?

That's a question for you to ask yourself. In the end, as an undergraduate in an accelerated program, you normally do cover the same academic ground as a standard pre-med student, so you're not being short-changed on academic knowledge. Also, for all GMed programs, the med school portion is never condensed. But proponents of the normal-paced 8-year GMed program think that you still need a full four undergraduate years to explore academic interests beyond medicine and to mature to the point that you can handle patients and accept the enormous responsibility of being a physician. Some agree, some don't. It's really up to you to decide how you feel about accelerated programs.

If you crunch all of your classes into 2-3 years, wouldn't that make your undergraduate courseload really intense?

Yes, more intense than a regular undergraduate curriculum, but nothing that a dedicated student can't handle. You'll still have some time to relax, pursue extracurricular activities, and get a taste of that quintessential college experience. Think of it this way: normal students who spend four years as undergraduates have *tons* of free time. Even if you were to double the courseload of those students, you'd still have a somewhat manageable schedule. (So maybe you'd attend 1.5 parties a week, instead of the normal 3.)

Some questions you probably have by now (and my attempt at answering them for you)

Is a GMed program for me?

If you in high school and are dead sure you want to get an MD, the answer is yes. If you are in high school and are *kind of* sure that you'd like an MD, then go ahead and apply to a few GMed programs. If you're accepted and decide to attend, but as an undergrad you figure out that medicine isn't for you, you can leave the GMed program and resume as a normal undergraduate, usually with no time lost or harm done.

As a GMed student, are you treated specially?

Yes. You get beaten up more often because everyone thinks you're a nerd (just kidding! . . . sort of). The serious answer is, in most cases, *no*. As an undergraduate student, you're treated as a normal undergraduate student. As a med student, you're treated as a normal med student. The only difference is you don't have to apply for med school or build your resume to do so (and if you're in an accelerated program, you might take a few special, condensed science courses). Also, while your friends are struggling to build their resume and losing sleep over the MCAT, you don't have to do any of that. Other than that, you're a pretty normal student. As such, if you decide medicine is not for you and you're an undergraduate in a GMed program, you can usually drop out of the program safely while continuing normal undergraduate studies at that college.

Are you forced to go to the med school that is affiliated with the undergraduate school, or can you apply to other med schools as well?

It varies from program to program. Some bind you to that one med school; others give you the freedom to apply to other med schools while still holding your guaranteed seat in the affiliated med school; and still others do something in between.

What's better, going to an Ivy (or near-Ivy) as an undergraduate, or going to some other school's GMed program? After all, if I can get into an Ivy, I'm probably good enough to get into med school in four years, right?

It's entirely up to you to decide if you want to attend a renowned school or a GMed program; usually you have to choose one or the other, because there's only a handful of high-status schools that offer GMed programs. If prestige is what matters to you, then go for the Ivy. If your desire to practice medicine outweighs your desire to have attended a fancy-pants school, then a GMed program is the safer option.

If you *do* go to an Ivy, be prepared to work your ass off for four years on building your resume, taking the MCAT, and trying to ace your classes to have a shot at getting into an American med school. Simply going to an Ivy as an undergraduate is *not* a guarantee of getting into a good med school, or any med school for that matter. Nonetheless, if you work incredibly hard, you certainly may end up at a better med school than you would be in had you gone to a GMed program instead. Keep in mind there is a small handful of esteemed schools that do offer GMed programs such as Rice, Caltech, Brown, Northwestern, Baylor, and a few others.

How to use the rest of this book

If you're still in the game, chances are you probably have a pretty good idea of what to do with this book: read it. Nothing too spectacular – sorry if you had your hopes up that I'd cover it all in the intro, and you could watch *Jersey Shore* reruns the rest of the afternoon.

But don't read it as if it were a storybook – that is, don't read it all through in one shot and then let it gather dust under the far corner of your bed. Instead, use it as a reference guide as you progress toward your senior year in high school. Skim through it once to get a sense of what's ahead for you. Then, reread it piece by piece as you move through high school and the application process, keeping track of what you've done and making sure you heed most of its suggestions.

Okay, now that we've covered the basics, we can finally work on turning you into a top-notch GMed applicant. Let's get this party started.

UNIT I

The Preparation Plan:
Building your resume and
demonstrating your passion
for medicine

INTRODUCTION TO THE NEXT FEW YEARS OF YOUR LIFE

THIS IS IT. If you've ever wondered what you'll be studying, who you'll be talking to, and how you'll be living your life for the next few years, the next 50 or so pages will give you a pretty good idea. The upcoming 5 chapters of this book make up a preparation plan that will guide you from middle school all the way through your senior year of high school. I've designed it not only to prepare you for the actual GMed application process in 12th grade, but also to *ensure that the process is as easy for you as possible.* To help you stay on track, I've included loads of tips and checklists in each section that you should go over before you move on to the next one.

If you're already years past some of these stages, not a problem. Just skim all the stages that you've passed (say, if you just bought this book and you're already in 11th grade, quickly read over the middle school, 9th grade, and 10th grade sections), make note of anything from those sections that you haven't done yet, and put them on your to-do list.

For most high school students, the college application season begins in late summer or early fall of senior year. If you follow this prep plan closely, here's what you'll have by then:

- Plenty of interesting, emotional, or sensational (or some combination thereof) medical and non-medical experiences and encounters that you've gathered through volunteering, internships, and other extracurricular activities. These stories will give you some good ideas when you're writing your college essays and preparing for your interviews.
- A handful of teachers, research mentors, volunteer supervisors, and other significant people who know you very well and think very highly of you, your work, and your personality. These are good go-to people when the time comes to ask for letters of recommendation.
- Good scores on all the standardized tests (like the SAT and SAT subject tests) that most GMed programs ask for.
- Good grades in all the right classes.
- An awesome resume.

A note on the resume

Of all the things listed above, the resume is arguably the most important. Although there is obviously no exact resume – no precise combination of awards, activities, and experiences – that could guarantee you a seat in a GMed program, there *is* one general resume template that works pretty well. Not only did I develop and follow this template myself, but I've also seen it work for a good number of other applicants. As such, the resume-building portions of this prep plan revolve around this template.

Overall, you'll want to have several *medical experiences* (like volunteering at a hospital or free clinic and shadowing a specialist) on your resume and also some solid *non-medical experiences* (like sports, chess club, the school newspaper, or other things along those lines).

You should further divide your "medical experiences" category into two sections: clinical experience (activities that involve some sort of patient interaction) and medical research experience (like a summer internship at a lab). It's nice to have a mix of the two to show that you can deal well with patients and are also comfortable with medical literature and science. However, without patient experience, you won't go very far in the application process. So if you have to choose between emphasizing one or the other, the safer bet is to go with clinical experience.

From a very general standpoint, your resume should have the following components:

- One or two big medicine-related projects – something bigger and better than anything else you've listed on your resume. A great research-related example of this would be publishing (as an author or co-author) one or more research papers in a medical journal or presenting a project at a medical conference alongside a research mentor. In the clinical realm, big medicine-related international (or domestic) service projects are usually looked upon quite favorably. Keep in mind that your "big project" can be either clinical – or research-oriented, and that you only need to do one or two of these projects – any more and it might look a tad unrealistic.

- Although a huge blob of little experiences in the hospital and the lab is nice (which is what most applicants will have on their resume), it's even better to give that blob some organization with one sensational, defining capstone project that you can easily talk at length about, write about, and put at the top of your resume to call attention to your application. There's tons more advice on how to formulate and develop your big project in the upcoming chapters.
- A few smaller medical experiences – things like volunteering at a local clinic or medical center, participating in a brief medical research internship, and shadowing or working for a physician. It's important to have more than just one medical experience to show interest and compatibility in all medicine-related settings.
- A few solid non-medical experiences, like volunteering in non-medical settings, playing a competitive sport, participating in debate tournaments, or playing an instrument in an orchestra. Whatever you do, it's important that you have something to show for your effort, like an award, publication, or some other form of recognition. This component of your resume is critical because admissions counselors want to make sure that you're at least somewhat well-rounded and have some interests and skills beyond the realm of medicine, even though medicine is your primary interest. Besides being well-rounded, even more important is that awards, publishing, and recognition demonstrate to admissions officers that you are 1) a self-starter, and 2) driven to succeed.
- Awards. Awards in anything – the science fair, an essay contest, National Merit, a history bee – are great to have no matter what you're applying for.
- Leadership positions in school clubs and, if possible, in community organizations. Once again, these are great to have for any application.

That's a quick look at what's ahead for you. Crying already? Grab a Kleenex and don't worry – you won't have to do all of these things at once. In the following sections I'll go into much greater detail and break all of these tasks up into nice little manageable pieces.

CHAPTER 2

What to do while you're in middle school

I KNOW WHAT you're thinking. *Is this dude for real? Is it really possible to start preparing for GMed programs as early as middle school?!* Well, now that you've spent your money on this book and are safely past the 30-day return policy, the real answer is . . . Well actually, it's *yes*. Yes, you *can* start preparing this early.

Keep in mind that, in high school, you'll be competing with thousands upon thousands of other high schoolers in the US that want a seat in a GMed program just as badly as you do. So how do you gain a competitive advantage over all those high schoolers? Get ahead before high school even starts. In middle school, you'll want to build *connections with the right people* so that it'll be easier to put together a resume with solid credentials in high school.

If you're already in high school and you're just reading this now, no worries! Although there are some great things you can do in middle school, you'll still be fine even if you don't do a single productive thing in 6th, 7th, or 8th grade. No one really cares what you did in middle school, as long as you don't commit a felony, or do anything else that might be documented on your school transcript in red ink, of course. Nonetheless, there are some great steps you can take in middle school to make sure that you're completely ready to go all-out on classes and activities when you move on to high school. Let's go over those steps now.

Middle school classes and grades

When you're a high school senior and admissions officers are reading over the dozens of applications you've submitted, it's highly, highly unlikely that they'll ever know – or even care – what you got in that one 7th grade history class with the cranky old teacher. In fact, chances are they won't see *anything* – any of your grades, activities, awards – from your middle school years. That's why everything you do in middle school should be done with the intent of preparing yourself to study hard and manage time well in high school. The best way to start preparing is, of course, to get good grades in your classes.

If you're going to a standard, whitewashed, cinder-block public middle school like the one I attended, it probably has a very fixed curriculum, allowing for no more than one or two electives each year in addition to the mandatory math, science, and language arts courses. So it must be really important to take advantage of those few electives, right? Wrong. *There's no need to load up on science electives if you don't want to.* If you'd rather be learning about sewing and cooking than circuits and simple machines, go for that home-ec class. Trust me, the consequences will be nil.

However, you shouldn't waste *all* of your time taking slacker courses. Many public high schools offer math, science, English, and foreign language courses that count for high school credit; if your middle school offers them, you should try to take – and get good grades in – as many of those as you can. Taking some of these courses (like Algebra 1, Geometry, and Spanish 1) will let you skip them in your freshman year of high school, so you can take more advanced courses (like Pre-calculus and Spanish 2). This will give you space in your later years of high school to take more AP or IB courses (like AP calculus or an AP foreign language class).

Extracurriculars

Again, hardly any – if any at all – of the activities you do in middle school will end up on your resume. But it couldn't hurt to get a taste of what you'll be doing in high school. That's why, as a middle school student, it would be a good idea to start looking into simple volunteer opportunities. It'll not only show your commitment to the community early-on, but it'll also make volunteer positions more easily available to you in high school.

In your free time, begin to take a look at the facilities in your community where you could be of some use, such as:

- homeless shelters
- assisted living homes
- clinics

- urgent care centers
- hospitals
- other places or organizations that might allow hands-on, human interaction-oriented volunteering (ew . . . not *that* kind of human interaction)

If possible, contact the volunteer department (or equivalent) of each institution and ask about volunteer opportunities: Are there any openings? What are the requirements for the position? Is any prior experience or training necessary? What kinds of jobs do the volunteers perform?

As a 13ish year-old middle school student, chances are you won't find very many places that will accept you as a volunteer; most of them will have minimum age requirements of about 15 or 16. But that shouldn't deter you from at least contacting the institution and asking about volunteer opportunities for the future. If you find yourself shut out by all the organizations in your area either by the age limit or by the fact that all positions have already been taken, *start talking to institutions that don't even offer formal volunteer opportunities.* For example, if there's an urgent care facility nearby that never really thought about opening itself up to volunteers, call up the receptionist and ask if you can help out at the facility with anything, even paperwork; you might be able to get a volunteer or shadowing position out of it. Since the urgent care center doesn't have any formal, publicized volunteer positions, it won't have any strict experience guidelines. However, make sure that your volunteering is safe and lawful; avoid doing anything clearly beyond your authority (like administering a vaccination or anything else that only trained professionals should do).

Since opportunities for middle school students are scarce, grab hold of any opportunity you can find, even if it's just a position at your local library. At this stage, just about any form of volunteering is great, because it'll 1) portray your dedication to community service, 2) count as prior volunteering experience that you can put on your applications for new volunteering positions in high school, and 3) help you make connections with fellow volunteers and members of volunteer departments. This last point is especially important because having connections within the volunteering community makes it easier to find and apply for new volunteering experiences. Stay in touch with these people – they are your future door-openers.

Looking ahead to high school

Most students aren't all that concerned when it comes to choosing a high school – they finish 8th grade at their district middle school, then move on to their district high school. Bada bing, bada boom. But if you're serious about applying to GMed programs, you'll want to be a bit pickier when choosing the school you'll be attending for the next four years. In the vast majority of cases, your district's public high school will be 100% fine. Still, you should double-check to make sure that the high school you'll be attending is accommodating to your ambitious resume-building and test-taking goals. Just remember that the goal is not necessarily to end up at the state's highest-ranked high school or the one with the coolest name, because GMed admissions counselors generally care neither for the name nor the reputation of the high school. Rather, the goal is to spend four years at a high school that offers all the resources and opportunities you need to be productive.

When you're in 6th, 7th, or early-8th grade, start to take a close look at your district's public school. In general, you want to ensure that the school's academic and extracurricular opportunities are ample and the atmosphere is right for you. Here's a list of some important things that you'll want to consider when assessing the school:

- **AP and IB courses:** A wide selection of AP (Advanced Placement) and/ or IB (International Baccalaureate) courses is by far the most important thing a high school can offer to its students; if your high school doesn't offer either of these, you should definitely start looking at some other secondary school options (more on this in a couple of pages). In high school, these advanced courses will not only boost your GPA, but will also show that you're ready for (and already have course credit for) college. Overall, they're great to have under your belt. But if you end up at a high school that doesn't offer AP or IB courses, it's not the end of the world. These schools sometimes notify colleges that they don't offer these courses (check with your counselor to be sure, though). In turn, colleges will partially forgive for your lackluster academic transcript, since it wasn't your fault that you weren't able to take any AP or IB courses. However, if you're at a school that offers AP and IB courses and you don't take any, your application won't look so hot; after all, you'll have no bona fide excuse for not taking any advanced courses.
- **Clubs and student organizations:** When it comes to clubs and other school-sponsored extracurriculars, it's important that your high school has three things: 1) a large and diverse group of student-run interest groups and clubs, 2) ample time for participating in those clubs, whether it's during the school day or after school, and 3) a simple process for organizing and starting new clubs. Since school clubs will be the primary avenue through which you will demonstrate leadership (yes, little ol' *you* will be leading a club) and entrepreneurship (yep, enterprising *you* will be founding a club), it's important to make sure the school has everything you need.
- **Sports and music:** If you're good at a particular sport or play a certain instrument in an orchestra or band, make sure that your school has

opportunities for you to pursue it further. Put simply, if you're a lacrosse prodigy, make sure the school has a lacrosse team. If you play the violin, make sure the school has an active orchestra. You don't want to drop a sport or instrument just because your school doesn't offer it; these sorts of talents can be garnered into resume – and essay-worthy activities and are great for maturity and personal development.

- **College prep support:** Most public high schools have some sort of "College and Career Center" – a place where students can consult knowledgeable staff and large databases for advice on finding scholarships, internships, and job opportunities. This information is incredibly useful – make sure your school has it available to students, whether it's through an actual "College and Career Center" or some other medium. And when you're in high school, use it as much as you can.
- **University affiliation:** Some high schools are affiliated with a community college, 4-year college, university, or other nearby post-secondary education institution. This partnership usually opens up the possibility of enrolling in some college-level courses, accessing extensive university libraries and databases, and doing lab work alongside professors and researchers.

Having some of the five things on this list (particularly the availability of AP or IB courses) at your side will definitely make it easier for you to prepare for the application process. But if, by the time you read this, you're already stuck at a high school that doesn't offer any of the five things listed above, you're fine. None of these things are 100% necessary for you to get into a GMed program.

In the end, the only thing that truly matters is *what you did* with your four years of high school: how hard you studied, how much effort you put into activities and academics. *Where* you had to attend high school isn't something that admissions officers are particularly interested in knowing.

If your government fails you . . .

What if your local government can't get its act together? Let's say the mayor blew all of your town's funds at Hooters and left the public schools with not a dime to spare. Let's say your district high school's genetics teacher is so inept, he thinks horseradish sauce is the result of a crossbreeding experiment between an equine and a root vegetable. To make a long story short, let's just say that, after comparing the list above to what your area public high school offers, you've just realized that you happen to live two blocks away from the lousiest high school ever built. What are you supposed to do now?

In all seriousness, this is a real possibility. If you find out that your district public high school doesn't offer either AP/IB courses or at least two other things on that list, then it might not be the best place to go about building a GMed-quality resume or transcript. But there's a way to solve this problem.

Start out by making a list of all the secondary schools in your area, excluding your district's school and any other regular public high schools outside of your district. List all the private high schools, regional magnet high schools, governor's schools (available in some states), and other college preparatory schools that you might be able to attend. Compare each of these schools to our list and make note of what each one does and doesn't offer. If you're considering a private school, take the tuition and associated costs into account, too.

Once you've done your analysis, it should be pretty easy to decide which high school is right for you. If that school happens to be one with a competitive application process (which is likely if you settle on a private or magnet high school), take a look at the school's application requirements. They may include things like scores on the SSAT (Secondary School Admission Test), letters of recommendation from middle school teachers, perhaps a short essay or two, and a list of your interests and activities. Give the applications for these schools a shot. If you don't end up attending the high school of your choice, not to worry – you still have a fine chance at getting into a GMed program. Once again, what matters is not specifically the high school itself; no, what makes all the difference on your GMed application is *what you did while you were there.*

Summary and checklist

- Do your best to get good grades in all of your classes.
- Take courses that count for high school credit.
- Find volunteering opportunities in your area.
- Make an informed decision on which high school in your area to attend, whether it's your district's public high school or some other school. Compare our *ideal list of offerings in this chapter* to what *each high school offers* to help you make a decision.

CHAPTER 3

What to do while you're in 9th grade

GREAT! YOU'RE FINALLY in high school. Before you start thinking about GMed programs, spend the first few weeks of school just trying to avoid the juniors and seniors – it's common practice for the upperclassmen to humiliate the freshmen by stuffing them into lockers, yanking up the waistband of their underwear from behind (the *original* snuggie), and playing other foul tricks (and if, heaven forbid, you're walking around with your nose in a *GMed book* of all things, you're twice as likely to be subjected to their depravity).

This chapter – What to do while you're in 9th grade – is arguably the most important part of this entire preparation plan. Why? Because no GMed admissions advice is good for just one year. Everything you learn in high school is good until that one culminating moment of your senior year, when you submit that very last GMed application at 11:59:59 PM on the day it's due. The advice you're about to read in this chapter should take up residence in the back of your mind for the next four years.

Therefore, I suggest that you legitimately re-read this chapter before moving on to any others (that's right, *legitimately* – sorry buddy, no Sparknotes for you). For example, when you're a junior and you finally decide to crack open the 11th grade chapter, review this chapter first. It'll remind you not only of anything you haven't done yet, but also of the activities that you need to *continue*.

Academics

The definitive guide to picking classes in high school

General advice

Unlike that of middle school, your high school curriculum is probably somewhat malleable; you might already have room for an elective or two this year. As such, there are some important tips you should keep in mind at the beginning of the year while deciding what classes to take. You should refer back to these tips not only in ninth grade, but also in subsequent years.

The first thing you should know is what you're trying to achieve. With respect to classes, your end goal is to build a very attractive academic transcript by the middle of senior year. A great looking transcript has the following qualities: a *large* preponderance of "A"s in the 25-or-so classes that you will have completed by the middle of 12th grade, and an *even larger* preponderance of "A"s (if not all "A"s) in just the BCPM (biology, chemistry, physics, and math) and English classes that you will have taken by then. Avoid grades of "B" or lower in any more than about 20% of *all* of your classes, and in any more than about 10% of your BCPM and English classes. Also, your transcript should show that you have gone up to the AP or IB level in six subjects: BCPM, English, and a foreign language (At a high school that doesn't offer AP or IB courses? See the "Looking Ahead to High School" section in Chapter 2.).

Based on these guidelines, pick your courses appropriately. In general, the few courses that you *are* able to pick should be solid, challenging courses (Remember home-ec from middle school? Sorry, none of those anymore.), but should not amount to an unreasonably hard courseload. Not only might you find your grades suffering, but you'll also have less time to devote to extracurriculars. Most of the electives that you have should be filled with BCPM, English, and foreign language courses to ensure that you reach the aforementioned end goal of going up to the AP or IB level in most of these subjects. Also keep in mind that, if you're focused specifically on *accelerated* medical programs (the 6 – or 7-year ones), taking *lots* of APs and IBs will help you place out of some introductory college courses and lighten up your condensed college courseload.

9th grade classes

Specifically for you freshmen: this is the year for you to figure out what your limit is – that is, the maximum amount of schoolwork you can handle while still fitting in some time for clubs and volunteer work.

If you have the opportunity to take an AP course as a freshman (that is, you have a free elective space and you've somehow completed the prerequisite for that particular AP), be cautious; you don't want to end up in a class that's too hard or have to take a College Board AP exam that you're not prepared for. Before signing up for the course, take a moment to skim through an AP exam prep book at the library. If the material seems familiar and you think getting an "A" in the class is more than just a remote possibility, sign up for the course – you'll be fine. Otherwise, put it aside until sophomore year or later. As it is, taking APs isn't your focus this year; since most of your mandatory freshman classes are simple and introductory-level, your goal should be to accumulate as many "A"s as possible to make your GPA solid before moving on to harder classes.

One last thing for you to do this year: begin charting out your academic plan for the rest of high school. Make note of all the elective spaces you'll have throughout high school and fill them with AP or IB English, foreign language, and BCPM classes, or their prerequisites. Try to squeeze in as many of them as you can *before* senior year, because colleges seldom see your senior year final grades until *after* you've been accepted or rejected.

A note on teachers

Hold it – before you finalize your course selection, there's one last thing you need to take into consideration: your instructors. There are a couple of things you should know about these people when it comes to picking classes:

- If you know of a teacher at your school who is notorious for giving out lousy grades (due to the bad-tempered nature of the teacher, not the difficulty of the course), avoid that instructor. Although it may sound shallow, the last thing you want on your transcript is an attention-hogging "C" or "D".
- It's unlikely that any of your ninth or 10th grade teachers will be writing your college recommendations. However, you may need to ask them for recommendations for any internships or volunteer positions that you'll be applying for this year or next. As such, you'll want to show these teachers – particularly the BCPM ones – that you're genuinely interested in the class and that you have a pleasant personality and a good work ethic.

Keeping an eye on standardized tests

Although the SAT and/or ACT will make up a big part of your application, there's no need to worry about preparing for them just yet. That can wait until sophomore year, or even the year after that. The SAT Subject Test, however, is something that will be hounding you every year of high school, regardless of whether you end up taking the SAT or the ACT later on. As you'll soon find out, most GMed programs require you to take a small handful of SAT Subject Tests in addition to the SAT. Some GMed programs exempt you from having to take one or two of these tests if you take the ACT instead, but you'll inevitably have to take a few.

SAT Subject Tests (formerly known as SAT II's) are one-hour long, multiple-choice tests on specific subjects like math, Spanish, French, physics, chemistry, German, world history . . . the list goes on (there are 20 tests on 20 different subjects). Each one has a maximum score of 800, kind of like one section on the real SAT. All of the tests require only one year's worth of introductory knowledge on the subject – that is, you'll be fine if you take the SAT Subject Test in Chemistry after you finish your high school's Chemistry 1 course. Of course, you'll be much more prepared if you also take an AP or IB level chemistry course before the test.

Although each GMed program asks for a slightly different set of SAT Subject Tests, there are five tests that, together, will satisfy the SAT Subject Test requirement for virtually any GMed program. These five are Math Level 2, Chemistry, Physics, any foreign language, and Biology E/M (There are two variations of the biology test: ecological and molecular. Either one is fine.). If you don't have time to take all five, at least take these three: Math Level 2, Chemistry, and Biology E/M; many GMed programs ask for *at least* these three, and you'll be able to apply to the majority of GMed programs without the physics or foreign language tests.

You should have scores of 700 or above for all of your SAT Subject Tests *before* the beginning of senior year. As a short-term goal, let's say that you should finish at least two SAT Subject Tests by the end of 10th grade.

Clubs, activities, and general resume-building

High school clubs

With respect to high school clubs, this year's assignment is pretty simple. Big officer positions in student organizations aren't often held by freshmen, so your mission this year is to build your credibility and reliability in certain clubs to a point at which other members are comfortable with electing you for office next year or the year after.

Early during your freshman year, get a sense of what kinds of clubs and organizations your school offers. If your counselor or the main office has a list of all the clubs at your school, take a look at it. Start to visit all of the clubs that interest you, and after a few weeks, begin to narrow your search. Pick anywhere from 2-5 clubs that you're genuinely interested in and think you could devote your after-school time to. Pick a mix of science, non-science, and service clubs; for example, a good assortment of clubs might include a chemistry club, a chess club, a theater arts club, and a community service club in which you might tutor young children, promote community environment clean-up programs, or record audio books for the blind.

Once you've chosen your 2-5 clubs, spend the rest of the year becoming an active, reliable member in each of them. Attend meetings, help out with projects and initiatives, and show that you're truly interested in the club. This way, when election season rolls around, other students will know who you are and acknowledge your efforts.

Founding a club

This year, you should put some thought into *founding* a club of your own at school or in your community – it's an awesome way to show initiative on your resume, and is also just a great personal learning experience.

Don't jump the gun by founding a school club during your freshman year without thinking it through. Instead, take your first year in high school to look at existing, well-established clubs, to learn how they operate, to develop a comprehensive idea of what your club's structure and function would be, and to find out the process for starting a new club in your school. This way, you'll have a good idea of what you're in for when you finally found your club in sophomore or junior year.

Come up with an idea for a club that addresses a need in your school or community – a club that actually has value when it exists. Here are some great examples of clubs and initiatives founded by some successful GMed applicants that I've talked to:

- One student noticed that science classrooms in nearby high schools are always short on lab equipment like pipettes and beakers, and never have any up-to-date equipment for students to use. She also noticed that some corporate labs in her area would always throw out perfectly good, unused lab equipment every few months. She founded a club in her community in which area high school students visited these laboratories, picked up the unused equipment before it was disposed of, and distributed it to high schools in the area.
- Across from one student's high school was an elementary school that didn't have enough resources to fund many after-school activities for its children. An avid chess player herself, she founded a club at her high school in which juniors and seniors would visit the elementary school every week to teach young children how to play chess and enroll them in local youth chess tournaments.
- One student, a volunteer at a local clinic, founded a club in his community in which high school students, clinic volunteers, and volunteer physicians would visit homeless shelters on weekends and offer simple medical attention to the poor.

- In one student's area was an annual neuroscience competition that was poorly attended by teenagers from her high school. She and a friend co-founded a school club that prepared students for the competition by helping them acquire the necessary knowledge, and signing them up for the yearly competition.

Volunteering

When you're a senior and the time finally comes to have that interview or write that essay, you'll want to be able to proudly say that you've been consistently volunteering for multiple years. As such, freshman year is perfect to get started on some volunteer work both within and beyond a medical setting. Although you can certainly ask your counselor and peers for any volunteer positions they know of, the process for finding and applying for volunteer positions in your area is pretty much the same as it was when you were in middle school (see the "Extracurriculars" section in the previous chapter). However, here are some new pointers that you should keep in mind this year:

- Don't volunteer at a hospital or clinic anymore if it means you'll only be filing papers and doing administrative work. That was permissible in middle school, but now you want primarily human interaction-oriented work.
- If you're having a hard time satisfying the first bullet, look for smaller institutions (free clinics and urgent care centers, for example); they're less likely to place stringent limits on your interaction with patients, physicians, and nurses.
- Look for any opportunities in your area to train for a high school volunteer EMT (emergency medical technician) position. Plan on enrolling in the training course as soon as you meet the age requirement; being an EMT is a great form of medical experience. Don't be dismayed if you can't find any such opportunities; high school EMT positions aren't available in all communities.
- Non-medical service is also a great, easy-to-find way to build your volunteering experience. If there's an opportunity in your area to help out at an assisted living home, serve at a homeless shelter, or tutor/mentor elementary school kids, go for it every week if you have the time.

Taking it all back to our master resume template

Before reading this section, go back to the very first part of this preparation plan ("An Introduction to the Next Few Years of Your Life") and review the part entitled "A Note on the Resume." Pay special attention to the components of the resume template. I'll wait . . .

Done? Good. Let's discuss each part of that template and figure out which components you still need to work on.

The big medicine-related project: Hold off on the "big project" this year; you don't want to take action before you're fully prepared, so take freshman year to come up with an idea for your project and to think it through. This year, start to look around and see what other students are doing, and if you know any current GMed students, ask them what they did. Based on what you learn, come up with a few rough ideas of what your "big project" might be.

Remember, if you plan on doing a research-oriented project, the course of action is relatively standard: after interning at a medical research lab during your sophomore or junior years or their respective summers, make it a point to co-author a publication on the research project you did in the lab alongside your mentor, present it at a conference, and/or submit it to a science competition like the science fair. That would count as your "big project."

But if you want to carry out a "big project" with a clinical bend, you might want to consider conducting some sort of large-scale health program either in the States or abroad. Taking part in the Borlaug-Ruan International Internship (a prestigious internship sponsored by the World Food Prize) or some other formal internship that addresses human health, for example, would seriously count as a "big project." If that doesn't work out, contact universities in the region you're interested in and look for faculty members who are interested in conducting a health project and are willing to let you work with them. If you'd rather carry out your project in the States, founding a community organization that somehow addresses the health of the needy or disadvantaged in your area would make a great big project. But regardless of whether you're doing a project in the US or abroad, understand that there are personal safety risks involved with working far away from home at your age. Just be careful, ya know?

Smaller medical experiences: If you're volunteering every week at a couple of local medical institutions as we discussed in the previous section, then you've got these small medical experiences covered. Keep up the volunteer work.

Non-medical experiences: If you haven't already, this is the year to pick up some other activities like a sport, debate, Model UN, competitive chess, some sort of job or internship in policy or politics, non-medical volunteering, or whatever else interests you. And as if I haven't said this enough: make sure you have something to *show* for your activities, some sort of recognition. It's one thing to put "played violin for three years in my basement" on your resume. It's another to put, "played violin for three years in front of large audiences, selected for district orchestra, and won second place in a state-wide violin competition."

Leadership: If you read the "High school clubs" section a few pages ago and you're regularly attending and participating in your 2-5 select clubs, then you don't need to worry about leadership for now. You'll reap the leadership-related benefits of your dedication to these clubs when you're elected for an officer position or two in sophomore or junior year.

Awards: Awards aren't something you should worry about just yet; opportunities to enter competitions will naturally come your way in a couple of years, when you have a ton of volunteering and research experience under your belt. Nonetheless, it couldn't hurt to try your hand at some contests this year. Stop by your school's College and Career Center or your counselor's office and ask for a list of reputable competitions, contests, and competitive scholarships for which you may be eligible. It doesn't matter whether they're on the local (usually the easiest), regional, state, or national level. Pick a few from the list (maybe one from each level) and . . . go for them. That's pretty much it. *Some popular national-level examples include:* the DuPont Challenge, Odyssey of the Mind, the Brain Bee, It's Academic, Science Bowl, Science Olympiad, and the American Mathematics Competition.

While you're doing all of this volunteering, researching, studying, and award-winning, there's just one last thing I'll ask you to do every year and every summer of high school: *keep track of everything you've done.* When you're a senior and it's time to put your official resume together, the last thing you'll want is to have forgotten half the things you've done over the past four years. So compile an ongoing list – a "resume-in-progress" of sorts – of *all* the activities you've done in high school; even the things that you think are only *remotely* worthy of a place on your resume. Also, keep note of any interesting or remarkable experiences you have, tasks you perform, or things you see; when it comes to writing college essays and having interviews, those anecdotes will be tremendously helpful.

Summer after 9ᵗʰ grade

This summer, apply for any formal research, shadowing, or clinical internships at universities, hospitals, and research institutions in your area. If you're barred from all of these formal opportunities because you're too young (most labs have a minimum age requirement of 16), try to organize an informal internship by contacting researchers at nearby universities, members of nearby research institutions, and physicians. Then ask them if they'd be willing to let you shadow or work under them. Whether you do it formally or informally, the important thing is that you get some sort of clinical or laboratory exposure this summer. This will make you a stronger applicant when you apply for more competitive internships in subsequent summers.

You should also spend your summer narrowing down your list of potential ideas for your "big project" and planning out the project carefully so you can begin to take action on it within the next year or so. And if, God forbid, you have any *free time* this summer . . . try to have some fun.

Summary and checklist

Academics

☐ Keep in mind that a competitive academic transcript has the following characteristics: 1) out of all classes, around 80% have "A"s, and 2) out of all BCPM and English classes, around 90% have "A"s.

☐ Fill most of your electives with BCPM, English, and foreign language courses so you can go up to the AP or IB level in all of these subjects.

☐ Gauge your preparedness carefully before taking an AP course during freshman year.

☐ Avoid taking classes taught by teachers who have a reputation for handing out low grades.

☐ Plan out how to fill your sophomore-, junior-, and senior-year electives so that you can go up to the AP or IB level in BCPM, English, and foreign language.

Standardized tests

☐ Before senior year, *definitely* take SAT Subject Tests in Biology E/M, Chemistry, and Math Level 2. If you think you'll do well and you have time, also take SAT Subject Tests in Physics and a foreign language.

☐ Take 2 SAT Subject Tests (with scores of 700 or higher) before the end of 10th grade.

Clubs, activities, and general resume-building

☐ Become an active member of 2-5 school clubs.

☐ Look for opportunities to found a club in your school or community.

☐ Come up with a few rough ideas for your big medical project.

☐ Fit some medical and non-medical volunteer work into your weekly schedule.

☐ Pick up a non-medical activity like chess, debate, sports, music, or any other skill that interests you.

- [ ] Try out for a few academic and science-related competitions.
- [ ] Compile an ongoing list of all the activities you've done and experiences you've had as a high school student.

Summer after 9th grade

- [ ] Get clinical and/or lab exposure through an internship.
- [ ] Develop your "big project" ideas further.

CHAPTER 4

What to do while you're in 10ᵗʰ grade

I F EACH GRADE in high school were a lollipop, 9ᵗʰ grade would be cherry flavor, 11ᵗʰ grade would be strawberry, 12ᵗʰ grade would be raspberry, and 10ᵗʰ grade . . . well, 10ᵗʰ grade would be that one defective lollipop that doesn't have any flavor.

If each grade in high school were a book, 9ᵗʰ grade would be *Harry Potter*, 11ᵗʰ grade would be *The Hunt for Red October*, 12ᵗʰ grade would be *The Da Vinci Code*, and 10ᵗʰ grade would be . . . *The Grapes of Wrath* (no offense, Steinbeck).

The point is, while your freshman, junior, and senior years in high school each have their own exciting characteristics, sophomore year just isn't as special. In 9ᵗʰ grade, you're getting acclimated to high school. In 11ᵗʰ grade, you're facing the brunt of high school academic and extracurricular work. In 12ᵗʰ grade, you're actually *applying* to GMed programs. In 10ᵗʰ grade, you're doing . . . just normal stuff, really.

That's why one of your goals this year should be to do everything you didn't do last year after reading Chapter 3. If the only volunteering you did last year was taking out the trash every Monday, now's the time to take up a volunteer position at a local clinic. If the only clubs you attended last year were nightclubs, it's time to join your school's debate team, buddy. If you haven't done *anything* yet, High School hath bestowed upon thee an extra year to get thine act together.

But it's not all *that* easy; there's still a number of new things that you'll have to work on this year if you want to stay ahead of the game. Let's take a look . . .

Academics

Classes

If you haven't already done so, pick your sophomore year classes with the help of "The definitive guide to picking classes in high school" in the Chapter 3. Although you should definitely sign up for at least one AP this year (preferably a BCPM, English, or foreign language AP), you shouldn't take any more than 2 APs as a sophomore unless you took an AP during freshman year and did reasonably well in the class and on the exam. Having to take three or more APs and AP exams as a sophomore with no prior experience in these types of courses might be a bit too overwhelming and time-consuming.

Standardized tests

Still antsy about the SAT and/or ACT? Hang tight – we'll start worrying about that a little bit later. In the meantime, I've got something else to quench your irrepressible desire to cram from Princeton Review books and bubble in College Board answer sheets: they're called SAT Subject Tests. Remember them?

If you'll recall, in Chapter 3 we decided that you'd finish two SAT Subject Tests with scores of 700 or above by the end of this year. If you already knocked one out at the end of freshman year, awesome. Regardless, you'll probably take at least one by the end of this year. But to make things a bit easier, take the SAT Subject Test in *June*, and sign up for the test that corresponds to the AP course you took this year. For example, if you took AP Chemistry this year, sign up for the June SAT Subject Test in Chemistry. That way you'll have taken the AP Chemistry exam just a few of weeks before you sit for the SAT Subject Test . . . and all that great chemistry knowledge will be fresh in your mind.

Clubs, activities, and general resume-building

High school clubs

Okay, so you spent all of your after-school time last year focusing on 2-5 clubs that you're interested in. Hopefully, by now, other members of the club acknowledge and appreciate the effort you've put in so far. Now it's time to reap the benefits of your hard work. That's right – this year, you're going for *officer* positions. Here's what you need to know to be successful:

First of all, there are two different types of school clubs. The first type is the national club: this club is usually just a school chapter of a well known national organization. This includes clubs like Relay for Life, Key Club, Red Cross, Junior State of America, National Honor Society, and most other honor societies. Student government, although not part of a large organization, belongs in this category because virtually every high school in the US has one. The second type is what we're going to call the school-specific club. This is a club that was probably founded by a student or teacher and doesn't exist beyond your school. An example would be a small student-run biology interest group at your school. National clubs are generally better-recognized than school-specific ones.

Secondly, try to run for legitimate positions – like president, vice president, treasurer, secretary, or historian – in which you'll make an important contribution to the club. If you're running for something like the Assistant to the Assistant Manager of Refreshments and Beverages just for the sake of having a position and a title, you won't gain much.

Thirdly, when you're preparing your election speeches, essays, and whatnot, you want to make sure that you're doing it for the right clubs. Ideally, you'll want to put on your resume that you hold positions in any combination of 1-3 national and/or school-specific clubs. Regardless of which combination you pick, split up the work: run for 1-2 positions this year and 1-2 positions in different clubs during junior year.

Finally, if you *are* elected to office this year, don't slack off. If you don't invest enough effort into the club as an officer, you might be ousted during the next election. This indicates a lack of commitment.

Founding a club

Another thing you should do this year is found a school or community club of your own, whether it's a new chapter of a national organization or your own school-specific club. If you spent freshman year looking around for club ideas, then you should have a pretty good picture of what your organization will do and how it will work. Your next step is to gather some support for the idea from students and faculty, make it an official club at your school, and then start building it.

If you still need to think through your club idea, take a look at the "Founding a club" section in Chapter 3 for tips and examples. If you don't think you'll be ready with a solid idea by the end of this year, not to worry – there's no rush. You'll still be fine if you wait until junior year to found the club.

Volunteering

As long as you continue the 1-2 medical and non-medical volunteering activities you started last year, you're all set in the volunteering category.

That said, make sure that you keep up *almost all* of the things that you started last year. Continue to pursue those non-medical interests you chose last year, whether they include dance, drama, or dog sledding (and again, remember to have something to *show* for them!). Also, keep on going for competitions in which you think you might stand a chance. If you weren't very successful with national competitions (like the DuPont Challenge) last year, go for some smaller-scale contests, like scholarships funded by local institutions. See your counselor or College and Career Center for more details on locally– or regionally-sponsored competitions.

Summer after 10th grade

If everything goes as planned, you'll take the SAT or ACT once or twice in junior year, and then, if necessary, you'll take it again in early senior year. So this summer is the perfect time to start preparing. Settle on a fixed preparation regimen, whether that involves signing up for a prep class or just working through a big fat prep book. If you're not sure whether to take the SAT or ACT, take practice tests for each to determine which one you're better at. If you score about the same in both, go for the SAT – it's more widely accepted among GMed programs.

Also, by now you should have a pretty good idea of what your "big project" is. So, this summer, in between SAT practice tests, you should start implementing it. If it's clinically-oriented, your first step will depend on what exactly your project is. But if it's a research-based project with the end goal of a publication, conference presentation, or something like that, your first step probably involves getting an internship and working on a project under a medical or biological research mentor. The person under whom you're working makes a huge impact on the outcome of your "big project." When you're applying for internships, *communicate with your potential research mentors* to help you decide which one will give you the best chance of working on a project you're interested in and making it something big.

Finally, take some time this summer to visit some nearby universities that offer GMed programs. Say, if you live within 1-2 hours' worth of driving from one of them, plan on wheeling down one day with a parent. A few weeks in advance, e-mail a small handful of GMed admissions counselors and current GMed students, asking if you could meet with them to discuss the program. During your meeting, just try to get a sense of what the program is like. How does it work? Is it difficult for students to preserve their guaranteed seat in med school? Do any of them lose interest in medicine during their undergraduate years? What do GMed admissions counselors look for in applicants? You'll probably be able to get the best answers to all of these questions from the students; keep their contact information for any questions you may have in the future.

Summary and checklist

Academics

- ☐ Take 1-2 APs this year.
- ☐ Finish 2 SAT Subject Tests by the end of this year. Sign up for the June SAT Subject Test that corresponds to the subject of the AP you took this year.

Clubs, activities, and general resume-building

- ☐ Run for officer positions in 1-2 school clubs.
- ☐ Found a school or community club this year.
- ☐ Keep up all the volunteer work and other activities that you started in freshman year.

Summer after 10th grade

- ☐ Prepare for the SAT or ACT.
- ☐ Start working on your big medical project.
- ☐ Visit nearby universities that offer GMed programs.
- ☐ Apply for medical research internships at nearby institutions. Even if your "big project" doesn't necessitate such an internship, these are great experiences to have and post on your resume.

CHAPTER 5

What to do while you're in 11th grade

D ELETE YOUR FACEBOOK account. Toss your cell phone out the window. Wipe your social calendar clean. Buckle down in the farthest, quietest corner of the library with your books (and perhaps a can or two of Red Bull) – because this year, you're going to be working hard. Hey, if it didn't require hard work, *everybody* would be a doctor! Junior year presents a peak opportunity to show GMed decision-makers that you've got *the right stuff*.

Traditionally, 11th grade is the year when you face the largest workload, in terms of both academics and extracurriculars. This year is critical because it's really your last chance to bolster your GPA and build your resume. You won't have much time during 12th grade to do those things because you'll be working on your applications. Although you'll be tweaking your credentials a bit over the summer, your goal should be to have a near-complete, application-quality resume and a solid transcript by the end of junior year.

Academics

Classes

Chances are you've spent the past two years in high school taking mostly introductory-level courses – intro to biology, chemistry, physics, perhaps some pre-calculus – that serve as prerequisites for more advanced courses. Now's your time to take advantage of that. This year, knock out as many AP-level BCPM/ English/foreign language courses as you reasonably can without overburdening yourself.

Also, look through your school's course catalog and make note of any interesting (and challenging) electives that it offers. Although course selection varies from school to school, many high schools now offer advanced classes with AP-level courses as prerequisites. For example, your school might offer a multivariable calculus, neuroscience, or artificial intelligence class with AP Calculus BC, AP Biology, or AP Computer Science as prerequisites, respectively. If you live near a college or university, you might even be able to take these advanced classes for college credit by enrolling as a part-time student; check with your counselor for details . . . as they say, *your results may vary*.

If possible, squeeze one or two of these quirky classes into your junior year schedule. But don't do it if you know it'll compromise your grade in another class – taking these high-level courses is by no means critical. The only purpose of this effort is to spice up your transcript: since many students applying to GMed programs (including you) will have taken a number of AP-level science and math courses, taking one or two more unorthodox classes will help differentiate you from your competitors.

The overall message is no different from what it has been in previous years:

1) Take challenging classes, and
2) Shoot for the best grades you can get.

For more advice on picking the right classes and setting up an appropriately demanding schedule, flip back to "The definitive guide to picking classes in high school" in Chapter 3.

A note on letters of recommendation

In senior year, when the time comes to fill out your applications, you'll want to use letters of recommendation (or "recs") from teachers who know you well and can accurately describe your interests, personality, and work ethic. A rec from someone who has only a vaguely distant memory of you will seldom work to your advantage. That's why – although there's no definitive rule – *it's usually a good idea to get your recs from teachers with whom you've worked during your junior year, summer after junior year, and/or early senior year*. A teacher you had in sophomore or freshman year probably won't recall enough experiences with you to write a thorough rec, unless you've somehow kept up with him or her over the years (through helping them out after school, working with them on an extracurricular activity, or something like that). If you've developed a good, lasting relationship with one of your teachers from 9th or 10th grade, it's probably fine to get a rec from him or her. Nonetheless, you'll still have to work on forging connections with your current teachers. Here's how you'll do it:

A month or two into junior year, once you've settled into all of your classes, get a sense of each of your teachers' personalities. Pick out the ones who appear open to making connections with students and get to know them better. Make an effort to participate more in their classes, talk to them after class, and get involved in any school organizations, clubs, or competitions that they sponsor. Ultimately, building relationships with teachers is almost entirely dependent on their involvement in other school activities, opportunities available to you to work with them, and their responsiveness to your efforts to build a connection. Since these 3 factors vary from teacher to teacher, do what you think is necessary to make them realize that their subjects matter to you.

Although it's great to build relationships with (and get recs from) teachers in all subjects, be sure to cover your bases first: establishing solid connections with *1-2 science teachers and an English teacher* should be your primary goal, since these are the two most common subjects that GMed programs require recs from. In addition, simply through active participation and hard work in all of your classes, you can ensure that most of your teachers will see you as a diligent student. Even if you're not their *favorite* student, respect from your teachers will prove to be extremely helpful if you ever need to ask for a last-minute rec from one of them during the application process.

As your junior year comes to a close around May/June, notify your 2-3 select teachers that you'd like them to write recs for you for the upcoming application season. It's important to be professional throughout the process: first ask them *in person* if they'd be willing to write a rec for you, then send them a "thank you" e-mail letting them know that you're grateful for their help and asking if there's anything you can do to help them write the rec.

For more tips on what you need to do to make sure that you get great recs from the right people, see the "Letters of recommendation" section in Chapter 11.

Standardized tests

The PSAT

Do innocent, everyday objects remind you of sadistic, perverted word problems or narratives you once encountered on a practice test? Do you talk excitedly with your friends about your scores on practice PSATs? (Trick question – it's junior year, you're not supposed to have time for any friends.) Do frantic thoughts about the PSAT occupy every moment of your consciousness? If so, you're not alone – currently, millions of juniors across the country are going hysterical over the PSAT. Let's investigate this fear-inciting, havoc-wreaking test a bit further.

You'll often see the PSAT written as the "PSAT/NMSQT" ("Preliminary SAT/National Merit Scholarship Qualifying Test"). It's simply an abridged version of the SAT – it has fewer sections, takes less time to complete, and is entirely multiple-choice (there's no essay), but its questions are at about the same level of difficulty as those on the real SAT.

The PSAT serves two primary purposes:

1) To help you gauge your preparedness for the actual SAT (although practice tests from SAT books are just as effective), and
2) To qualify for a chance to earn a National Merit Scholarship.

Here's a bit more on that scholarship:

Every year, a national cutoff for the PSAT is determined (usually around 210, or the equivalent of a 2100 on the real SAT) based on the performance of all juniors who took the exam that year. If you score above the cutoff, you'll be granted entry into a competitive application process for a limited number of National Merit Scholarships, each worth $2,500. This scholarship is nice to have for two reasons:

1) It'll help you cover some of your college expenses, and
2) It's a neat little thing to put on your resume.

While it's a nice thing to have when you're applying to GMed programs, it is absolutely not essential – largely because:

- Med school admissions committees sometimes aren't as familiar with National Merit as undergraduate admissions committees are, and
- It doesn't reveal as much about your interest in science/medicine as, say, an award at the state science fair does.

So sure, if you score above the cutoff, go ahead and give the scholarship application process your best shot – it couldn't hurt to add "National Merit Scholarship Recipient" to your resume; and hey, who doesn't love free money? But if you *don't* score high enough, and you *don't* get to stick it on your resume, don't let it bother you even for a second.

The bottom line is this: the PSAT is just a way to help you see how well you're prepared for the real SAT. If you do well, great – keep up your SAT practice regimen. If you don't do so hot, don't panic – just be sure to put extra effort into preparing for the real SAT. And since your score doesn't go to any college (or anywhere else you wouldn't want it to go) without your expressed permission, you have even less reason to worry about the PSAT. Conclusion? *As long as you don't bomb it, the PSAT really doesn't matter.*

SAT Subject Tests

By the end of this year, you should have completed all the SAT Subject Tests that you plan on submitting with your GMed applications. Keep in mind that getting a score of 700 or above on the Math Level 2, Chemistry, and Biology E/M tests comes first; if you have time, take the Physics and (any) foreign language tests as well.

The SAT and the ACT

Hopefully you prepared well last summer and throughout the school year, because now it's time to take the real SAT or ACT. *(Not sure which one to take? Flip back to the "Summer after 10th grade" section in Chapter 4 for some advice.)* You should plan on sitting for the exam at least once (but not more than twice) during your junior year. If you're still not satisfied with your scores from your second sitting, you should have time at the very beginning of your senior year to take it for the third and final time. As a junior, take the exam during the second half of the school year – that way you'll have had time to receive your PSAT scores, assess your results, and brush up on any of your weaknesses that they exposed.

After you get your results from your first SAT/ACT, the first thing you need to do is figure out how well you did. You've probably heard this before – "there is no magic SAT or ACT score" – and although that may be valid for most undergraduate programs, it only retains half of its truth for GMed programs. Many of them have hard-and-fast cutoffs for the SAT/ACT – it varies from program to program, but typically falls somewhere between 1800-2200 for the SAT and 28-33 for the ACT. Your final, overall SAT/ACT score (regardless of how many times you took it) must be at or above that cutoff for you to even *submit* an application to that particular GMed program. For example, all applicants for the University of Miami's GMed program (called the Honors Program in Medicine) must have at least a 1400 on the math and reading sections of the SAT or a 32 on the ACT.

GMed programs that employ this system usually claim that they're not concerned with your exact score as long as it's at or above the cutoff. That is, once they've checked to make sure that you scored higher than their required minimum, they toss your SAT/ACT score out the window and focus on the other parts of your application. Although it's possible that they may return to your SAT/ACT score and take a look at the breakdown of your results, the chances of that happening are pretty slim.

For the remaining GMed programs that don't have a minimum SAT/ACT score requirement, there really is no magic number – you could get almost any score (as long as it's not absolutely dreadful) and still have a chance at landing a seat in that GMed program. Nonetheless, the higher your score, the more favorably you will be looked upon. Brown University's Program in Liberal Medical Education is one of many GMed programs that do not enforce a score cutoff. Just as a very general guide for these types of programs: if you have anything above a 2200 on the SAT or 32 on the ACT, you're pretty much in the clear.

Clubs, activities, and general resume-building

The "big project"

Now that you've spent the past couple of summers developing your idea for your big project (the main headline on your resume), you should now have a very detailed plan of what your "big project" will be, whether it will be clinically – or research-oriented, and how you plan on putting it together. *(Don't have a clue what I'm talking about? See "A note on the resume" at the very beginning of Unit I for a refresher.)* If you're ahead of the game, you may have already phased in the early stages of your "big project" during the summer before 11th grade.

This year, you're going to bring this project into full swing. If it's more of a *research project* (i.e., the results of some medical research internship you did last summer), you should start looking into conferences where you can present your work, journals that will publish your research, competitions that you can enter, and any other ways to make your research project BIG. If it's a *clinical project*, you should be well into the process of implementing your project plan. Regardless of what your project is, you should plan on it occupying the bulk of your out-of-school time this year.

Awards and competitions

You know that uncle of yours? The really wealthy one who drives around Beverly Hills in his Ferrari all day long? Every family seems to have one: a filthy rich, market-savvy uncle who's made a living turning money into more money. Well now it's *your* turn to be the rich uncle. But in this case, you'll be turning each one of the items on your resume into much more.

Over the past couple of years, you've gathered lots of resume-worthy experiences: you've volunteered, done research, gotten good grades, founded and led student organizations . . . I could go on forever. What's so great about all of these things is that they're exactly what most competitions and contests available to you are looking for. In short, now that you've done all these things, it's time to capitalize on their potential to make you a good candidate for scholarships and awards.

If you were involved in some sort of biology – or medicine-related research through an internship last summer, a great way to capitalize on that research is to use it as an entry for the science fair or any other science competitions in your area. Awards at the school, regional, state, or international levels of Intel's annual science and engineering fair (commonly referred to as ISEF) are all great to have on your resume.

Likewise, local companies and societies often offer competitive scholarships for students in the area. The fact that you have lots of great activities backing you up makes you an excellent candidate for them.

Remember to consult your school's "College and Career Center" or your counselor for reputable contests, competitions, and scholarships that you may qualify for. Give any national, state, or local competition a shot, provided that:

1) You qualify for entry,
2) You think that your chances of landing some sort of award are more than just nominal, and, most importantly,
3) *The time you spend on it doesn't unduly interfere with your schoolwork or any of your extracurriculars.*

Clubs, activities, and everything else

While you're working on your "big project" and competing for awards and scholarships, don't forget to keep up with all of your other important activities. Continue to volunteer on a regular basis. If you feel as if you don't have enough medical volunteer work under your belt, or you think your current volunteer position is becoming too dry, *mid – to late-junior year is just about the last chance you have to add or switch volunteer positions* while still having enough time before application season to show commitment to your new position. Switching any later – say, just a month or two before the beginning of senior year – would make it seem as though your new position is just a short-lived stint (perhaps even a stunt) rather than a long, meaningful experience. The same applies to any medical work or shadowing activities that you're continuing.

Be sure to keep up with all of your non-medical activities, as well. If you're on the debate team, the school orchestra, or the lacrosse team, don't let up on the tournaments, concerts, or games – only then will you be able to show that you're still committed to those activities.

Deciding where to apply

Another important thing you'll be doing this year is figuring out which GMed programs you want to apply to. Although you won't have your *final* list by the end of junior year, you will have a pretty good idea of which programs are the top candidates for that list. *Doing this will make it much easier for you to direct your academic and extracurricular efforts toward the requirements and expectations of those specific programs.* For example, if the Caltech-UCSD Medical Scholars Program is at the top of your list, you'll know that you need to build a research-heavy resume.

This year, give some thought to which GMed programs you'd like to attend. Here's a great way to get started:

1) Begin by making a long list of all the GMed programs that even remotely interest you. This list should be based on some very elementary criteria. For example, if taking the MCAT is the last thing you'd ever want to spend 4 hours and 25 minutes of your precious life on, then list only the GMed programs that don't require you to take the MCAT (this list will end up being pretty long – it may even go up to 30+ programs). *Flipping through the Appendix at the back of this book is a great way to get this list started and learn about the most basic factors that differentiate GMed programs from one another.*

2) In your spare time, do some more in-depth research on each program (and its respective undergraduate and medical schools) on your list. The best way to do this is to peruse each program's website thoroughly, read conversations on CollegeConfidential.com, and consult any other internet resources you can find. If possible, get in contact with a student currently in the program – they might be able to give you some valuable insider information on what the program is like. Attending college fairs in your area can be helpful, too.

3) As you learn more about each program, slowly begin to cross out the ones you dislike and highlight the ones you would really like to attend. You should make these decisions based on more specific, personal criteria. Things you might want to consider include: the length of the program (6, 7, or 8 years), tuition and other expenses, any undergraduate minimum GPA requirements for matriculation to med school, any limitations on what you can major in as an undergrad, the reputation of the undergraduate school and the medical school, weather, location, size of the school, the undergraduate curriculum . . . the list goes on. Literally anything that matters to you is fair game.

4) Continue this process throughout the year; by the end of your junior year, your list should be down to about 20 programs.

This list is nowhere near final – you'll be doing much more work with it over the summer. Nonetheless, being familiar with 20 GMed programs that you're really interested in will make things much easier for you during the application process. For example, if one of these programs asks for a rec from a teacher in an unexpected subject, you'll know to ask that instructor in advance. Or, if one of your programs looks for something really unique in its applicants, you'll know it well ahead of time so you can tailor your application materials to that program's liking. Any way you slice it, making a tentative list of GMed programs ahead of time is a smart move.

Summer after 11th grade

Phew! Junior year is finally out of the way. Now, with the one summer you have left before the beginning of application season, you're going to slowly transition from the resume-building phase to a new phase that revolves around planning and completing your GMed applications. *So this summer, you're going to be working on both your resume and your apps.*

Your resume

As you begin to wind down on your efforts to build your CV, there's just a handful of things that you need to take care of before summer's end:

- If you haven't already done so over the past couple of years, participate in a biological or medical research internship over break. This summer is your last chance to show that you've experienced not only the clinical, but also the research side of medicine. If you've done research in the past, see if you can work in the same lab again this summer. If not, apply for internships at other labs in your area. Either way, doing research over the summer is a great way to show your continuing interest in medicine.
- Be sure to continue all of your medical and non-medical activities throughout the summer.
- Wrap up your "big project" by the end of this summer – by then, you will have hopefully worked on it long enough to make it the most impressive item on your resume.
- Take a preliminary glance through the next unit of this book (entitled "The Application Process") to give yourself an idea of what to expect during the application season. If you come across anything that you might be able to take care of this summer – like formatting your resume or submitting transcript requests – get working on it.

Your applications

Letters of recommendation

Near the end of your junior year, you should have notified at least 3 teachers that you would like them to write recs for you. But keep in mind that teachers aren't the only ones who are allowed to write recs – in fact, if you were to submit recs *only* from teachers, your application might come across a bit dull. Recs from people who can attest to your commitment to research, community service, or some other aspect of medicine (in combination with teacher recs) will give an application reader a better sense of the kind of person you are.

So, this summer, think of any doctors you've shadowed, medical researchers you've interned with, or volunteer supervisors you've worked under recently. If you've established a strong, ongoing relationship with any of them and you think that they'd be able to write you a detailed, positive rec, *be sure to give them a heads up*. Non-teacher recs from just 1-2 people should be plenty.

Finalizing your list of GMed programs

During your junior year, you came up with a list of about 20 GMed programs which were under heavy consideration for applying. Well, pull out that list again, because it's time to do some shortening. Continue to do in-depth research on each of these programs and, based on specific, personal criteria, eliminate the ones you no longer find desirable. *(Need some help shortening the list? Flip back to steps 2 and 3 in the "Deciding where to apply" section of this chapter. Also check out Chapter 9: Where to apply.)*

You should continue to narrow down the list until you have anywhere between 5-15 remaining programs that you're seriously interested in. The exact number of programs on this list really depends on how many you want to apply to. If you're more of the "GMed or bust" type – that is, you're not interested in attending anything other than a GMed program – you'll probably want to have about 15 schools on your list. But if you're not so sure that GMed programs are the perfect match for you, keep it to about 5 schools; all the other places you apply to will just be normal undergraduate programs. BUT . . . (this is important) regardless of how many programs end up on this list, be sure that *you meet all of the SAT/ACT score cutoffs, minimum GPA and class rank requirements, and any other academic constraints for every program on that list*. If you don't, you might not be able to apply!

This list of 5-15 schools will be the *final list of GMed programs* that you'll be applying to – although it might not be 100% final yet. In Chapter 9 of this book, we'll do a quick safety check to make sure you're applying to more than just the high-profile, high-risk programs.

The first thing you're going to do with your final list is to squeeze as much information out of it as you can so there are no surprises when application season finally begins. Here's how you'll do that:

First, on a spreadsheet, document the application submission deadlines (and any other significant dates) of every program on your final list – important dates should be clearly stated on each program's website. Be sure to familiarize yourself with *when* these due dates are, *the order* in which they fall, and the number of days you have *in between* each deadline.

Then, download a copy of the application for each GMed program. In most cases, the entire application will consist of:

1) The Common App (on the Common App website, www.commonapp.org),
2) The undergraduate supplement (also on the Common App website), and
3) The GMed program supplement (available on either the Common App website or the program's website).

In other cases, the application will be entirely available on the program's website or on the Common App website and will consist of slightly different components.

Read through each application, making note of how demanding each one appears to be. In Chapter 10 you'll decide on the order in which you'll tackle your applications, based on the difficulty of each one, the submission deadlines, and the relative importance of each program to you.

Finally, brainstorm essay topics this summer. As you read over each application, you may notice that every single one of them inevitably has the following essay question (or some variant): "Why do you want to be a doctor?" or "Why medicine?" Give some thought to how you can answer this question in about 1 page – it might help to pull out your compilation of notable experiences from over the years if you're in need of ideas. *(Don't remember what I'm talking about? Reread the very last part of the "Taking it all back to our master resume template" section in Chapter 3.)* Although you don't have to produce a draft just yet, at least come up with detailed outlines for a few different ways in which you might develop this essay. Once you've finished that, do the same for any other common essay topic themes that you notice on your undergraduate or GMed supplements. If you have time, start to turn these outlines into drafts and give them to your friends and family members for feedback. But if you're in a time crunch, don't worry – in Unit II, we'll officially begin to work on your essays.

Visiting schools

Now that you know which schools have made it to your final list, it's time to make sure that *they* know who *you* are. One of the most critical things you should do this summer is to actually visit the schools that you're most interested in – the small handful of GMed programs at the very top of your final list. I'm not talking about those standard college visits where you go on a campus tour, buy a college shirt for mom and pop, and head home – I mean serious visits where you'll meet with GMed faculty, students, and admissions counselors.

The purpose of these meetings is twofold. The obvious one is to learn more about the GMed programs you're most interested in – what these programs' undergrad and med schools are like, and what they expect from their applicants.

The other purpose is a bit more subtle. You see, during the application season, a GMed admissions officer will probably end up reading recs, resumes, and essays from *hundreds* of applicants whose names mean absolutely nothing to him or her. He or she might vaguely remember that "Katie Jones's" essay was about volunteering at some shelter and that it was slightly more interesting than "John Anderson's" essay about shadowing a *podiatrist*, but who cares?? A paper application supplies hardly enough information to make a proper judgment on who's the more qualified applicant. In most cases, your application will just appear to be *marginally* more impressive than the rest.

But if an admissions officer comes across a recognizable name, from having met him or her face to face, that counselor will automatically devote more attention to – and, later on, more precisely recall the details of – that application. Say an officer comes across the file of an applicant named "Jayson Marwaha" (what a coincidence!). Even before reading Jayson's application, the officer will think to him – or herself, "Oh yeah, I remember Jayson – he visited the admissions office this summer and asked me some smart questions. He must be really interested." Consequently, Jayson's application will be more *significant* – will mean *more* – than the application from any other faceless high schooler. As such, the second (and more discreet) purpose of these meetings is to leave a good impression with the decision makers and ensure that they get a strong sense of your interest in their program.

But before you go on these visits, there's some planning to be done:

1) Select up to 5 GMed programs from your final list that you're most interested in. It's likely that you may have to take a plane to visit some of these. If you're up for that, great. Otherwise, no worries – just visit the GMed programs on your final list that are within driving distance.

2) Send emails to GMed faculty and staff, saying that you're interested in their program and would like to meet with someone to find out more (you might be able to get these e-mail addresses from the university's website, or through a connection you have at the university). Also ask if there are any students currently in the program that you could meet with – this way, you'll learn more about the students' general opinions of

the program. Ideally, you should set up meetings with 1-2 GMed faculty members and/or admissions officers and 1-2 students.

3) Prepare a list of intelligent questions about the program and its principles, culture, and atmosphere. And of course, also have some questions (but not too many) about what the program looks for in its applicants. During your meeting, be sure to use your questions as a way to engage the faculty member/student in a pleasant conversation about the program – don't just rapid-fire your questions at him or her.

4) Afterwards, send each person you met with (including the students) a "thank you" e-mail. And if you're not already broke from all the plane tickets, feel free to buy yourself a university t-shirt, pendant, or beer mug from the campus bookstore (for the record, if you decide to buy a beer mug, it was *your own* idea).

Summary and checklist

Academics

☐ Take as many AP-level BCPM/English/foreign language courses as you can without overburdening yourself. Like Clint Eastwood (aka Dirty Harry) said, "A man's gotta know his limitations."

☐ If you didn't get that joke, watch *Magnum Force* (1973) with Clint Eastwood.

☐ If you can, take one or two unusual, advanced courses this year, either at your high school or at a nearby college.

☐ At the end of the year, notify 1-2 science teachers and an English teacher that you would like them to write recs for you.

Standardized tests

☐ Take the PSAT. If you do well, great – give the National Merit Scholarship competition a shot. If you don't score above the National Merit cutoff, don't sweat it – just brush up on your skills so you're more prepared for the real SAT.

☐ Aim to score 700 or above on at least the Biology E/M, Chemistry, and Math Level 2 SAT Subject Tests by the end of this year.

☐ Take the SAT or ACT 1-2 times this year. A score of 2200 or above on the SAT or 32 or above on the ACT will likely clear the minimum score requirement for GMed programs that use a cutoff, and is also a solid, competitive score for GMed programs that don't.

Clubs, activities, and general resume-building

- ☐ Bring your big project into full swing this year.
- ☐ Partake in competitions, contests, and scholarships. Be sure to make use of things you've already done in the past – for example, if you did research last summer, present your work at the science fair.
- ☐ Don't forget to keep up with your volunteering, medical, and non-medical activities.
- ☐ Based on a combination of both objective criteria and personal reasons, develop a list of about 20 GMed programs that you're interested in applying to.

Summer after 11th grade

- ☐ Get involved in a medical research internship.
- ☐ Continue all of your ongoing medical and non-medical activities.
- ☐ Wrap up your big project by the end of the summer.
- ☐ Skim through Unit II: The Application Process.
- ☐ Notify 1-2 "non-teachers" (i.e., volunteer supervisors, research mentors, or doctors you've shadowed) that you'd like them to write recs for you.
- ☐ Narrow down your list of 20 schools to around 15 if you're sure you want to attend a GMed program, or about 5 schools if you're not so sure.
- ☐ Familiarize yourself with the submission deadlines, essay prompts, and application requirements for each program on your list.
- ☐ Brainstorm ways to answer the ever-prevalent "Why medicine?" essay question and any other common essay prompts.
- ☐ Meet with key faculty members, admissions officers, and students from your top 5 GMed programs to give them a sense of who you are and to learn valuable info about their programs.

CHAPTER 6

What to do while you're in 12ᵗʰ grade

8 PAGES – THAT'S it. Just 8 pages from now you'll be relieved of every resume-building, standardized test-taking, late night-studying, library-inhabiting duty that you've had to deal with since freshman year. This chapter is only 8 pages long for a very simple reason: *there's very little left to be done this year in the way of preparation.* Your resume, your academic transcript, and heck, even your high school career are all quickly approaching completion. Aside from some simple issues that you'll have to clear up at the beginning of the year (which make up the primary topic of this chapter), this preparation plan has nothing left to throw at you. Congrats – you win.

But, in my perennial quest to raise your spirits, I'm here to tell you that this chapter makes up not even a quarter of what you'll be doing this year. If you *really* want to find out "What to do while you're in 12ᵗʰ grade," check out Unit II: The Application Process, which begins at the end of this chapter – you'll have to deal with every word of it.

If that doesn't make you ecstatic enough, here's one other thing to keep in mind: at the very beginning of your senior year, be sure to take action on the advice not only in this chapter, but also in the first 4 chapters of Unit II. Since there's a bit of preparatory work to be done before you actually start filling out your apps, getting an early start on that unit will definitely pay off.

Academics

Classes

When it comes to selecting senior year courses, it's important to strike a fine balance between easy classes (to ensure that schoolwork doesn't override the amount of time you have to work on apps) and challenging classes (to show colleges that you're still a strong student). If there are any AP-level BCPM/English/foreign language courses that you haven't taken yet, pick 1-2 of them this year. If there are any less intense, non-science AP-level courses (like AP Micro – or Macroeconomics or AP U.S. Government) or moderately challenging science electives that interest you, take some of those as well. Overall, the difficulty of your first semester courseload should be on par with that of your junior year courseload. But feel free to make your second semester schedule slightly less demanding by filling the gaps between your APs with some less-taxing semester-long electives.

During the first semester, it's critical that you get *the best grades you possibly can in all of your classes* – your first semester senior grades make up the *last* set of grades (and, arguably, the most heavily scrutinized set of grades) reported to your colleges before admissions decisions go out. Although second semester grades are also important, they are less so because colleges see these *after* they've made their decisions. Nonetheless, if admissions officers notice a *significant* drop in these grades (or in the difficulty of your classes) relative to your past academic performance, your admission could be rescinded. Even though the likelihood of this happening to any student is low, stay on your toes, and keep those grades up.

Standardized tests

Last year, you should have taken the SAT or ACT 1-2 times. If you're not satisfied with your scores from those sittings, you should consider taking the exam once more this year. *(Refer to the "Standardized tests" section of Chapter 5 for some guidelines on the kind of score you should be shooting for.)* If you *do* decide to take it again this year, register for the earliest exam date available, which usually falls in September or October; you don't want to have to worry about standardized tests in November, when you're hard at work on your apps.

Also be sure to have completed all of your SAT Subject Tests by no later than a couple of months into your senior year. If you haven't scored 700 or above on the Biology E/M, Chemistry, and Math Level 2 exams, take care of those as soon as possible. If you haven't taken the Physics or foreign language exams yet, don't worry about them anymore – focusing on your apps will be a much better use of your time.

Clubs, activities, and general resume-building

Although your applications may be incredibly time-consuming, it's important to make sure that you fulfill your duties and obligations in the clubs you hold officer positions in, at the institutions you volunteer in, and in any other medical and non-medical activities that you've listed on your resume.

Staying on top of your extracurriculars throughout the application season is crucial because it wouldn't look too cool if your resume showed that you abruptly quit volunteering, shadowing, swimming, or playing the violin at the beginning of senior year. That might very well leave application readers with the impression that you've been doing all these things not out of personal interest or for self-betterment, but rather just to be able to slap it on your resume. When it comes to your extracurriculars, the bottom line is: keep up with business as usual, and you'll be fine.

The Intel Science Talent Search and the Siemens Competition: To compete or not to compete?

Perhaps the biggest (and probably the last) two resume-building opportunities you'll have this year are the Intel STS (Science Talent Search) and the Siemens Competition. Both are national science competitions open only to high school seniors, and both are regarded as incredibly prestigious. Awards granted by both competitions not only have large monetary values (the top prize for both competitions is $100,000), but are also coveted by thousands of high school seniors and respected by thousands of educational institutions around the country. Put simply, there's a lot of hype around both of these competitions every year. As such, you may notice that some of your friends are entering one or both of them.

Both the Intel STS and the Siemens Competition very closely resemble ISEF, the Intel-sponsored science fair, in that:

1) You must have conducted an independent scientific research project in order to enter, and
2) The quality of that project and your presentation of it determine how far you advance within the competition.

Although a few discrepancies come into play at the national level of each competition, these two principles remain the same.

It's possible that, if you did a medical research internship over the past couple of summers, you may have a project that is eligible for entry. If not, just skip this section. But if so, give careful consideration to whether or not you want to compete, because this decision could affect the quality of your GMed apps. Here are some things to consider:

- If you decide to compete, you might as well enter STS *and* Siemens. Although there's a lot of writing and paperwork involved in both, the rules and requirements for each are so similar that entering the second one is much easier after having done all the paperwork for the first.
- The entry deadlines for both competitions fall right in the middle of application season, when you'll be hard at work on your GMed apps.
- The work involved with entering both competitions combined is just as time-consuming as about 1 full GMed app, essays and all.
- Placing as a Siemens regional finalist, a Siemens semifinalist, or an STS semifinalist (or higher) is thought of highly by GMed programs that value research experience, but even more so by most normal undergraduate degree programs.
- Since awards from these competitions don't speak as well to your interest in medicine as they do to your talent for academic research, GMed programs aren't terribly focused on them. Nonetheless, they still look great on your GMed app.

Still not sure what to do? Here are answers to some important questions you might have:

Will recognition from the STS and/or Siemens competitions make me a more competitive GMed applicant?

Absolutely – especially if you make it to at least the Siemens regional finalist or STS semifinalist round. But keep in mind that it probably doesn't mean as much to a GMed admissions officer at your state university as it might mean to an officer at MIT or Princeton.

Will STS and/or Siemens recognition (or a lack thereof) alone determine whether or not I get a seat in my favorite GMed program?

Probably not.

Is it that "one special thing" that GMed admissions counselors are looking for?

Absolutely not.

Is it possible for a solid application without any STS/Siemens recognition to be equally competitive or more competitive than an application with one of those awards?

Absolutely!

In conclusion, you *should* enter STS and Siemens if:

1) You think you stand a chance at getting some sort of recognition or award (unfortunately, this is a very subjective decision), and more importantly,
2) You think you have enough *time*. It won't do you much good to slap an STS/Siemens award on your resume if it means you had to sacrifice the time necessary to create a really enthralling "Why medicine?" essay.

As such, if you think entering STS/Siemens might negatively affect the quality of your GMed apps on almost any level, it's probably not a good idea.

But regardless of what decision you make, you still have my vote of confidence. If you've been following this prep plan from start to finish, don't worry – your application will be rock-solid.

Summary and checklist

Academics

☐ Fill your first semester schedule with moderately challenging classes, such as AP-level BCPM/English/foreign language courses, advanced science electives, and non-science AP-level courses.

☐ Make sure your first semester grades are as good as ever.

☐ Feel free to take things a bit easier during your second semester of senior year, but avoid: 1) precipitous drops in your grades, 2) dropping year-long classes that you took during your first semester, and 3) filling your entire schedule with easy classes.

☐ If you're not satisfied with your SAT or ACT scores from junior year, take the exam once more this year.

☐ Take any outstanding SAT Subject Tests within the first couple of months of your senior year. By then, be sure to have scored 700 or above on at least the Biology E/M, Chemistry, and Math Level 2 exams.

Clubs, activities, and general resume-building

☐ Continue to participate in all of your usual extracurriculars, including volunteering positions, clubs in which you hold an officer position, and all of your other regular medical and non-medical activities.

A special note on the Intel STS and the Siemens Competition

☐ If you have a research project that is eligible for the Siemens Competition and/or the Intel STS, give careful consideration to whether or not you want to participate. If 1) you think you stand a chance, and 2) the time you invest in these competitions won't negatively impact the quality of your applications, then you should indeed give them a shot.

UNIT II

The Application Process

INTRODUCTION

IF YOU WATCH enough TV, you've probably already noticed this common phenomenon: whenever announcers use the phrase "If you're just joining us . . ." and try to fill you in in less than a sentence, they're never fully able to capture the true essence of what you really missed. The phrase works neither for nature shows ("If you're just joining us . . . the cute little baby penguin is dead.") nor for football games ("If you're just joining us . . . Janet Jackson's halftime show was cut short."). So criticize me all you want, but just this once – since I suspect that this will be a starting point for many last-minute readers – I'm going to have to use that phrase:

If you've finally cracked this book open, you're a high school senior, and you're just joining us now . . . you missed the entire Preparation Plan. That's right – at least four years' worth of tips and tricks on building a solid resume and picking the right schools. The good news is that you can still craft a really sweet GMed application with just the chapters in Unit II. So in the interest of time, you should start reading from here.

Not to worry, though – all that advice in the Prep Plan hasn't gone to waste! When you have time, quickly skim Unit I. That'll introduce you to the jargon I've been using (like "big project" and "little non-medical activities") and the things I expect you to have already done as a freshman, sophomore, and junior. That way, you'll be able to use the advice in the upcoming chapters much more effectively.

Also, a quick note to both the new readers and the ones who've been here all along: although GMed app deadlines may seem distant, the application season for you begins now – at the beginning of 12th grade. GMed submission due dates are often awkwardly scheduled, and crafting polished applications takes time, so you should begin reading this unit and working on your apps on the very first day of your senior year.

CHAPTER 7

Overview and timeline:
What to expect from GMed apps

THERE SHOULD BE laws regulating locker room behavior. Seriously. I have no experience with women's locker rooms, but I can at least tell you that this problem is growing out of control in men's locker rooms worldwide: there's no standard protocol or code of ethics governing locker room conduct, so every man just does whatever the hell he wants.

Some guys are overly self-conscious, so they undress in isolated corners and pull the complex gym-shorts-under-your-suit-pants maneuver so as to not expose an inch of skin while changing into work-out clothes. Other guys at least have the decency to wrap a towel around their waist before coming out of the shower. And then there are the conceited old guys who stroll around butt-naked, flaunting their stuff as if they're expecting an ancient Greek artist to appear and carve a stone sculpture of them. There's just no single established way to behave in the locker room.

Interestingly enough, GMed programs are no different. Unlike normal undergraduate programs, which all have similar application components (usually the Common App plus an undergraduate supplement) and similar deadlines (virtually 90% of college app due dates fall on January 1), GMed programs are so far and few between that each of them end up making their own deadlines, application parts, and admissions processes however the heck they want. Here's my attempt at explaining all of these rules as succinctly as possible:

Application components

The written application

As you begin to download and look at the apps for the programs you plan on applying to, you'll notice that there are 3 common ways in which most programs choose to structure their applications:

Case 1

Some applications will be made up of 3 separate components: the Common App, an undergraduate supplement, and a GMed supplement.

The Common App is a relatively simple online application that you'll fill out just once and submit to all of the schools you apply to. If you haven't seen it already, make an account on the Common App website (www.commonapp.org) and take a look – it's where you'll put your full resume, some of your other most basic credentials, and one essay on any topic of your choosing.

The undergraduate supplement, also available on the Common App website, is specific to each school. It usually asks one or two essay questions specific to that university – usually something along the lines of "Why do you want to attend [this school]?" or "What in particular about [this school] interests you the most?" – and sometimes asks you to elaborate upon an item in your resume. In rare cases, a GMed program won't require an undergraduate supplement (like Drexel's BA/BS/MD program, which only asks for the Common App and the GMed supplement), but most schools will ask you to submit it to ensure that you're interested in both the actual undergraduate school *and* its GMed program.

The GMed supplement, usually accessible only on the school's website, will probe deepest into the medical experiences on your resume. It will have 1-3 essay prompts, one of which will inevitably be along the lines of *"Why medicine?"* or *"Why do you want to be a doctor?"* The remaining prompts will be a bit more unorthodox. Some examples include: *"Describe an adversity you once faced and how you handled it," "What are your most important strengths and weaknesses?"*, and *"Outside of medicine, what are some of your other most passionate interests?"*

The Rice/Baylor Medical Scholars Program is an example of a GMed program that uses the 3-component format. Rice/Baylor MSP requires you to submit 1) the Common App and the Rice University undergrad supplement through the Common App website, and 2) the Rice/Baylor MSP supplement via snail mail.

Case 2

Some GMed apps only have 2 components since they combine the undergraduate supplement and the GMed supplement into 1 document; the content of these apps is usually no different from that of their 3-component counterparts. The applications for Brown University's Program in Liberal Medical Education and Boston University's Liberal Arts/Medical Program are both good examples: in addition to the Common App and each school's respective undergraduate supplement, you must fill out an additional GMed section and answer 1-2 medicine-related essay questions located at the bottom of the undergrad supplement.

Case 3

A small handful of GMed programs out there have 1-component applications that are entirely separate from the Common App or any other applications for regular undergraduate admission. Although usually shorter than 2 – or 3-component applications, these apps still analyze your entire resume and ask essay questions that cover a wide range of topics, including your interest in medicine, the undergraduate school, and the GMed program. One program that uses this type of application is NEOMED (Northeast Ohio Medical University) and its 3 affiliated undergraduate schools (University of Akron, Kent State University, and Youngstown State University).

These aren't the *only* 3 formats in which GMed apps come, but they *are* the most common. Even within these 3 types of applications, there's a substantial amount of variability. For example, some programs with 2 – and 3-component applications (like the Caltech/UCSD Medical Scholars Program and University of Pittsburgh's GMed program) only release the GMed supplement in December or January to those who applied early to the undergraduate school and were accepted. *As such, be sure to visit the website for each program you plan on applying to and familiarize yourself with the way its app is structured.*

Interviews

After you've submitted all of your written application materials, the GMed committee reviews them – but not for admission. Based on the quality of these submitted documents, they'll determine whether or not they want to extend to you *an opportunity to be interviewed on-campus by faculty, staff, and students currently in the program.* Only extremely qualified applicants are selected for interviews: from the couple thousand seniors that apply to the more popular GMed programs, only around 100 applicants (or approximately twice the number of students they plan to admit) are invited. In turn, from that pool of 100 interviewed candidates, usually between 30 and 50 are actually offered admission to the GMed program. As such, if you don't make it to the interview stage, you won't be able to land a seat in that program.

For each GMed program that you're selected to interview at, you'll be invited to visit the campus for a day or two to conduct anywhere from 1-4 interviews with a combination of med school faculty, undergraduate faculty, admissions officers, and GMed students – again, the structure and format varies between different programs. *(More tips on how these interviews work and how to ace them in Chapter 13.)* Unfortunately, this is a "no expenses paid" invitation – you'll have to front the money for the plane ticket and any other travel costs.

After your interviews, members of the admissions committee will assess your performance on them; about a month later, they'll release their final acceptance or rejection letters. In many cases, that decision is based on more than just how much the committee took a liking to you during your interview: they may also take a second look at your written app to help them select the best cohort. Nonetheless, *your interview performance almost always plays the most significant role in determining whether or not you make it past the final part of the application process.*

In summary, the entire application process consists of two cuts: the first one determines your eligibility for on-campus interviews and is based on the quality of your written application. The second (and final) cut determines whether you've been accepted or rejected from the GMed program, and is mostly (if not entirely) based on your interviews. Sometimes your written app is considered again, sometimes it isn't – but regardless, *the interviews are almost always more important for the second cut.*

Timeline

Here's a schedule of all the above events:

Written Applications

Deadlines for all written application materials – including the Common App, undergraduate supplements, and GMed supplements – as well as the (typically optional) undergraduate alumni interviews fall anytime between early September and late January. The 3 most common due dates for these materials are around November 1, December 1, and January 1.

After you submit these items, the admissions committee will review your application and determine whether or not they'd like to invite you for on-campus interviews.

Interviews

Between mid-January and mid-February, you'll be notified by each program via snail mail or e-mail if you've made it past the first cut and have been selected for the interview stage. If chosen, you'll also be asked to select your interview date from a list of options, all of which are placed throughout February and early- to mid-March. You may have to take a plane or a train to interview on campuses far from home – which means, if you're invited to several interviews, you might have to buy a lot of tickets!

Notification

No later than about 2 months after your interview date, you'll hear back from the GMed admissions committee regarding its decision to either admit or reject you. Most inform you in late-March and others around early-April. Only a small handful of programs actually notify you on April 1, the most commonly-used notification date for regular undergraduate programs.

Interestingly enough, some GMed programs inform you of their final decision as early as 2 weeks after your interview date. This only further emphasizes the point I mentioned in the previous section: the outcome of your interview is more important than the quality of your written application in determining whether or not you make it past the second and final cut. In these programs, it appears as though members of the admissions committee quickly convene after all candidates have been interviewed and make their decisions based on those results.

Summary

- There are 3 general types of GMed applications:

    - 3-component apps that consist of the Common App (or something similar, if the school doesn't accept the Common App), an undergraduate supplement, and a GMed supplement.
    - 2-component apps that combine the undergraduate and GMed supplements into 1 document.
    - 1-component apps that use one special document just for GMed applicants

- How the interview process works:

  - The quality of your written app determines whether or not you're invited for on-campus interviews.
  - In most cases, about 50% of interview candidates are admitted to the GMed program (so if the committee plans to admit 30 students, 60 will be called for interviews).
  - Both your written materials and your interview performance (but mostly the latter) are reviewed to determine whether or not you make it past the final cut.

- Approximate timeline:

  - Written application deadlines fall anywhere between September and January; many fall on November 1, December 1, and January 1.
  - Interview invitations go out in January and early February.
  - On-campus interviews take place in February and March.
  - GMed acceptance notifications go out around late March and early April.

CHAPTER 8

What happens after you submit your application, and how the review process works

"@#$%!!! I forgot to put my name on it!"

I F THAT'S THE first thing that resonates throughout your entire neighborhood after you submit your written app online, then perhaps I should've included a Chapter 7½ entitled "Dogs mark their territory, so should you" (warning: urinating on your laptop may result in electrocution . . . and a smelly laptop).

But regardless of what profanities you choose to shout out, what happens on *your* end after you click the "submit" button is totally up to you. You could treat yourself to something nice at Starbucks, throw a party, get right back to that 10-page AP Gov paper due tomorrow, or feverishly check the mailbox for your interview invitation (I guarantee you it won't be there yet) – it really doesn't matter.

On the other hand, for the schools you're applying to, receiving your application is just the beginning of the long *review process* – the procedure the school staff follows to evaluate your personality, skills, and credentials and ultimately to determine whether or not they want to offer you a seat in their GMed program.

Up until now I've been referring to the group of people who make admission and rejection decisions as the "GMed admissions committee." For all you care, these "committees" could be almost anything – even secret societies whose members wear hooded robes and use age-old bone-scattering and constellation-reading traditions to help them decide whom to admit. It's now time to clarify who these people are and how they review your application. Knowing what your essay-readers and interviewers are like will help you market yourself accordingly.

The review process

There are probably dozens of different procedures that schools follow to evaluate your app. However, the two processes described below are the most common and most representative; many other methods differ only slightly from these two.

Process 1

Once you submit all the necessary components of your GMed application, this is what might happen on the other end:

1) The undergraduate admissions committee (the same committee that evaluates all the normal applicants for the school's undergraduate program) reads through your undergrad app materials, including the Common App, the undergrad supplement, and any comments submitted by your undergraduate alumni interviewers.

2) If they like your application, they'll forward your file to the GMed admissions committee (usually made up of some combination of med school admissions officers, med school faculty, undergrad admissions officers, and undergrad faculty). They may even notify you early of your admission to the undergraduate school.

3) The GMed admissions committee reads through all of your materials, but scrutinizes your GMed supplement much more closely than any of your other documents.

4) If the GMed admissions committee considers you as one of its top applicants, you'll receive an invitation for on-campus interviews with GMed faculty and students. Note that it is not possible to get an interview invitation if the undergraduate committee doesn't like your application.

5) After your on-campus interviews, members of the GMed admissions committee convene to decide which applicants they want to admit to the GMed program.

6) Around late-March or early-April, the GMed committee will notify you of their final decision. You'll also receive the undergrad admissions committee's decision around that time if you haven't already.

Process 2

Alternatively, in some other schools, the GMed admissions committee is the first to weigh in on your application. In that case, this is what the review process looks like:

1) The GMed admissions committee reads through your materials, focusing primarily on the content of your GMed supplement and any other medicine-related materials you submitted.
2) If they don't like your application, they'll bump your files down to the undergraduate admissions committee. At that point, only the undergrad committee will review your app; you'll no longer be considered for admission to the GMed program.
3) But if the GMed committee *does* like your application, they'll invite you for on-campus interviews. Afterwards, they'll make their final decisions. Those whom they admit to the GMed program are automatically granted undergraduate admission as well. The interviewees whom they reject from the GMed program are then considered by the undergrad committee for admission to the school's regular undergraduate degree program.
4) Around late-March or early-April, you'll receive the final decisions from both the GMed and the undergraduate admissions committees.

The common element in both processes is that you're considered for both GMed admission and regular undergraduate admission independently. So while it obviously isn't possible to be admitted to the GMed program but rejected from the undergraduate school, the reverse is certainly possible. That is, it's possible to still be accepted by, say, Northwestern, and attend the university as a normal undergraduate student, even if you weren't admitted to HPME (Northwestern's GMed program).

Another important point to remember is that, since more or less the same people end up reviewing your application regardless of the process, neither pathway is more favorable to you that the other. As such, this information should not affect which schools you apply to – in most cases, you won't know which process any given GMed program uses until *after* you apply.

Summary

- There are two general ways in which schools review apps from GMed applicants:

  - In one review process, the undergraduate admissions committee receives your materials first, and forwards them to the GMed admissions committee after they've made sure that you're qualified for undergraduate admission.
  - In the other process, the GMed committee carries a bit more authority. They review your GMed materials first – if they're not too thrilled with your application, they'll bump it down to the undergrad committee. Otherwise, if you make it past the interviews and earn admission to the GMed program, you also earn undergraduate admission by default.

- Neither process is more advantageous to you than the other.
- Both processes make it possible for you to earn admission to the undergraduate degree program even if you're rejected by the GMed program.

CHAPTER 9

Where to apply:
Putting the final tweaks on your list of schools

NEAR THE END of your junior year, you should have given some thought to which and how many GMed programs you want to apply to. If you're just starting your list from scratch, here's what you need to do before developing the final list of GMed programs to which you'll be applying:

A quick recap from Chapter 5:
Coming up with a preliminary list of schools

A great way to begin thinking about potential schools is to skim through the appendix of this book – it'll introduce you to some of the most elementary characteristics and defining features of GMed programs, like undergraduate GPA requirements and limitations on what you can major in. Pick out a few of these factors that matter to you – these will be the black-and-white, objective criteria that will define every school on your list. Proceed to make a (very long) list of every school in the appendix that fits these criteria. For example, if you don't ever want to take the MCAT, only include programs that don't require a certain MCAT score for matriculation to med school.

Now do some more in-depth research on each school and begin to eliminate the ones that you're no longer interested in. This process of elimination should be based on subjective criteria that are important to you, like your preferred undergraduate curriculum, the school's reputation, your college tuition budget, or even location and weather. *Also be sure to eliminate schools that have academic constraints that you haven't fulfilled, like certain SAT/ACT score cutoffs or minimum GPA requirements.*

By the end of this process, you should have a list of 5-15 schools that you're interested in; closer to 15 if you're sure you want to attend a GMed program, and closer to 5 if you aren't.

Safety checks: Making sure your list of schools is *smart*

Now that you have a fairly detailed plan of where you want to apply, you just need to run a few "safety checks" to ensure that you're apply to a wise combination of schools – not just haphazardly to the ones you find peripherally interesting. The two checks you'll do will ensure that:

1) You won't overtax yourself (with only the most demanding apps) to a point at which the quality of each application begins to degrade, and
2) You don't end up applying just to the most competitive and most sought-after GMed programs.

Safety check 1: Is my workload manageable?

The last thing you'd ever want to do is to try to carry more than you can handle. Sure, applying to a bajillion GMed programs might increase your chances of landing a seat in one of them, but not if you don't have enough time to do a good job on all of them. It's absolutely critical to make sure you're working on the right *type* and *number* of apps.

By now, you should have already created a Common App account and downloaded blank apps for all the programs you intend on applying to. As you begin to tailor your resume and draft your essays *(more advice on all of that in the upcoming chapters)*, start to discriminate each app based on its relative difficulty. This involves making note of a few things:

1) Any overlapping essay topics between two or more apps (i.e., if apps for three schools ask you to write something along the lines of how you overcame a personal "challenge" or "adversity," you might be able to use the same essay three times with only minor changes to each),
2) Anything unusual that each app requires (like an abnormally large number of essays), and
3) The amount of time between each deadline (to help you figure out how many apps you'll need to work on at one time).

Based on these observations, if you notice any unreasonably demanding apps or any difficult ones with back-to-back (or identical) due dates, ask yourself: "Will I be able to handle this?" If the answer is an obvious *"no,"* feel free to *substitute* 1-2 schools on your list for ones with easier and less-demanding apps (avoid lengthening or shortening your list at this point). But if the answer isn't as clear, leave them on your list for now – when the heat of application season sets in and the due date comes closer, you'll have a much better idea of what you can and can't do.

Safety check 2: Am I applying to the right mix of "safe" and "risky" programs?

If you're a diehard GMed fan and you plan on applying to a ton of programs, it's imperative to make sure that you're applying to a *smart* combination of them. Coveted as they may be, don't just apply to the high-profile ones like Northwestern HPME, Brown PLME, and Rice-Baylor MSP – if your #1 priority is to earn a guaranteed seat in med school, then you should also consider programs that aren't as well-known or as competitive.

Begin this safety check by determining the relative "riskiness" of the programs on your list. A good place to start is acceptance rates: these percentages (or the numbers needed to calculate them) are almost always available on programs' websites, CollegeConfidential.com, or somewhere else on the World Wide Web. Compare acceptance rates for each program on your list to those of some "tier 1" programs (like Northwestern HPME or either of the other two listed above). That'll give you a sense of how competitive the ones on your list are.

Another factor to consider is the prestige of each program's undergraduate and medical schools. By nature, if the reputation (and correspondingly, the *rank*) of the med school and/or the undergraduate school for any given program is very high, the GMed program will probably be quite difficult to get into.

Based on this information, play around with your list until it looks something like this ideal one:

What a strategic list of schools looks like

- 3-5 "risky," or very competitive, programs that you're interested in *(some examples include: Northwestern HPME, Brown PLME, Rice-Baylor MSP, the USC Baccalaureate/MD program, CalTech-UCSD MSP, University of Rochester REMS, and the University of Pittsburgh GMed program)*,
- 3-5 moderately competitive programs that you're interested in *(for example: the Union-Albany Leadership in Medicine program, the VCU GMed program, the GW BA/MD program, Boston University's Liberal Arts/Medical Program, and the Penn State-Jefferson Premedical-Medical program)*, and

- 3-5 "safe," or relatively less competitive, programs that you're interested in *(like Drexel's BA/BS/MD program, UMKC's BA/MD program, and NEOUCOM's BS/MD program)*. Avoid thinking of these schools as your "safeties" – there's really no such thing as a "safety" GMed program, since all of them are incredibly hard to get into. These "safe" programs are intended to be the ones on your list that you have the *highest likelihood of gaining acceptance to* and are included to ensure that you have a respectable chance at landing a seat in at least one program.
- Finally, adding 2-3 regular undergraduate programs to your list couldn't hurt.

A note on normal undergraduate programs

That's right, it's not a mistake – I just threw 2-3 regular undergraduate schools onto your list. As much as I'm sure you detest those *standard, boring* undergrad programs, applying to at least a couple of them is an absolute must. The concept of "safety" does not exist – I repeat, *does not exist* – in the realm of GMed programs. Statistically speaking, the chances of any given student landing a seat in one of them are so low that *no one* – not even a baby genius who won the Nobel Prize in Medicine at age 3 – is guaranteed admission to a GMed program. As such, these 2-3 undergrad schools will serve as your safeties. In the cataclysmic event that you don't get into *any* GMed programs, these schools are there to make sure that you'll at least be able to go to college and apply to med school the regular way.

The definition of a "safety school" is one that you're about 90% sure you'll be accepted to. Accordingly, just pick schools that you know are very easy to gain admission to – preferably in-state, public universities with subsidized tuition rates, so you won't be paying much if you *do* end up having to attend. Feel free to tack on any additional undergraduate schools with quick, easy apps as you see fit. However, keep this in mind: since most schools consider their GMed applicants for both GMed admission and undergraduate admission separately, *almost every one of your GMed apps is also an app to an undergraduate program.* So don't overload on the undergraduate "safeties" – just be prudent and apply to 2-3.

And finally, if you also want to apply to 1-2 very prestigious schools like Harvard or Stanford for reasons of personal pride, go ahead. Just remember that, when push comes to shove and your GMed deadlines are quickly approaching, finishing the apps for these fancy undergraduate schools should *not* be your top priority.

Some advice for the rest of you

If you aren't dead set on getting into a GMed program and you only plan on applying to about 5 of them, your list will be much easier to make. Simply apply to the 5 programs in which you're most interested, regardless of each program's prestige or acceptance rate. If you just want to apply to the big-name programs like Rice-Baylor MSP and Caltech-UCSD MSP, that's totally fine – since you aren't 100% sure if you even want to attend a GMed program, you might as well disregard the "relatively less competitive" ones and just apply to the ones you like the most.

If that concerns you a bit, not to worry – you're safeties are still covered, since you'll probably end up applying to 5-6 regular undergraduate programs on top of those GMed programs. Just be sure that your list of regular undergrad programs contains a good mix not only of "reach" schools like the Ivies, but also of *safety* schools (remember the 90% rule?) like in-state public universities.

Conclusion

And there you have it – after all the research, elimination, and safety checks, you now have your official *final list of schools*. Be warned, though – this may not be the exact list of schools that you'll end up submitting applications to. If time becomes an issue, you may have to do some last-minute shortening of your list just a day or two before submission deadlines. More details on that in the upcoming pages.

Summary

- Once you've developed your list of about 15 GMed programs, you need to check for two features to make sure your list is smart:
- Safety check 1: Is my workload manageable?

  - If you notice any difficult apps with overlapping due dates and you don't think you'll be able to handle that workload, feel free to substitute 1-2 programs on your list for ones with less demanding apps. Try not to reduce the size of your list, though.

- Safety check 2: Am I applying to the right mix of "safe" and "risky" programs?

  - The ideal GMed program list has 3-5 "risky" programs, 3-5 moderately competitive programs, and 3-5 less competitive programs.
  - You should also apply to 2-3 (preferably in-state) regular undergraduate schools that you're at least 90% sure you'll earn admission to. These will be your safety schools.

- If your GMed list only has about 5 programs, just apply to the ones that you're most interested in. Also be sure to apply to the right mix of 5-6 undergraduate schools.

CHAPTER 10

Where do I start?!?:
How to handle all the work

A T THIS POINT in the process, it's only natural to feel a bit overwhelmed. When you add up all the things you need to do before submitting your apps – all the essays that need to be written, all the transcripts and recs that need to be sent, all the paperwork that needs to be filled – it amounts to a pretty hefty load of work. And jumping into that mess with your eyes closed will only make things worse. This chapter is especially important because it'll guide you through a great way to begin tackling your apps, help you stay organized and focused throughout the entire process, and teach you how to allocate your time sensibly.

Before going any further, do the following 4 things: (*These have all been mentioned in previous chapters, so if you've been keeping up, you should be all set.*)

- Set up a Common App account.
- Download *all* of the apps that you plan on submitting.
- Get a feeling for the difficulty of each app, taking things like the types of essay prompts, number of essays, and any unusual requirements into account.

- On a calendar, make note of all deadlines (and any other important dates) for every GMed program and normal undergraduate program that you plan on applying to.

Your 3-step, kick-app strategy

Now that you've gathered all of your apps and documented all of your deadlines, you have all the information you need to best manage all of the work. Here's a 3-part, time-saving strategy that uses this information to help you figure out *what you should be doing at every moment of the application season*. To give you an idea of the timeframe for this strategy, you should have made it through Steps 1 and 2 by the very beginning of the school year, and should be well into step 3 no later than the first or second week of senior year (of course, the earlier you start, the better).

Step 1: Getting the menial stuff outta the way

If you think essays are the only things that contribute to the infamy and overall lameness of the application season, you're wrong. Not only will you have to spend countless hours in front of a computer writing dozens of "insightful" essays, but you'll also have to do tons of mindless work. That's right – for the next few months, you'll be stamp-licking, transcript-ordering, envelope-sealing, post office-visiting, and admissions office-calling yourself into oblivion.

Two very tedious – yet very essential – tasks that you should take care of early-on are sending your *standardized test scores* (from the SAT, ACT, SAT Subject Tests, etc.) and *copies of your academic transcript* to each of your schools. Sending test scores shouldn't be too much of a hassle – just visit the College Board and/or ACT website and place your orders. But, if your high school is anything like mine was, ordering transcripts might be a bit more complicated – picture one poor old lady in the main office drowning in ceiling-high stacks of transcript request forms and on the verge of a nervous breakdown.

You have to be careful when sending official transcripts through your high school. First of all, the process varies a bit from school to school, so be sure to consult your counselor or your high school's website for the correct protocol. Chances are you'll have to fill out a request form and give it to a member of the school staff, who will send your official transcripts to the appropriate colleges. Submit these requests ASAP.

Secondly, since high schools aren't usually prepared to handle such large volumes of requests, there's a decent chance that this one poor old lady I was telling you about (the one person who sends out *all* of the official transcripts for every senior in your high school) will forget to send a few of yours out, mail them out late, or just lose your request form altogether. So, a few weeks after you submit this form, be sure to give each of your schools' admissions offices a call to ask them if they've received your official transcript.

If you take care of your test score reports and official transcripts well ahead of time, you'll be able to work on your essays uninterrupted.

Step 2: Prioritization

As you were recording all of your submission deadlines on a calendar, you may have noticed that these due dates often converge around certain days – November 1, December 1, and January 1, in particular. Although it *is* a bit frightening to have several apps due at the beginning of every month for 3 consecutive months, there's an easy way to handle it: prioritizing the schools that fall on each due date. Here's what you'll do:

Take a look at your calendar of deadlines again. If 3 or more apps fall on – or within a day or two of – the same due date, rank those programs in terms of how important they are to you. For the purposes of this step, this ranking will also determine the order in which you complete each school's app and the amount of time and dedication that goes into each one.

Listing each app that falls on the same deadline in order of importance is a fail-safe way to make sure that the apps for your favorite schools get done first and receive the most attention. Also, in the event that you run out of time before finishing all of your apps, this method ensures that the ones you aren't able to submit are only for your low-priority schools. But just as a precaution, *be sure to place at least a couple of your "safe" GMed programs high on your list*, leaving them at the bottom puts you at risk for not having the time to apply to any of them.

As an example of this prioritization exercise, consider the following scenario:

An example of how to prioritize

It's around late-August and you take a look at your calendar. You notice that you have 5 apps due on December 1 for the following GMed programs: University of Rochester REMS, Boston University's Liberal Arts/Medical Program, Rice-Baylor MSP, the George Washington BA/MD program, and Drexel's BA/BS/MD program. You decide to work on these apps in the following order:

1) Drexel BA/BS/MD program: Drexel is at the top of your list because it's one of your "safe" GMed programs. Although it's not your favorite program, you know that it's a smart idea to work on this app first and have your bases covered before focusing on the more "risky" programs.

2) Rice-Baylor MSP: After you finish Drexel's app, you'll immediately start working on your Rice-Baylor application. Since this program is one of

your top favorites, you want to make sure you have enough time to do a great job on this app.

3)   University of Rochester REMS: You simply list the remaining 3 programs (Rochester, Boston, and GW) in order of decreasing interest.

4)   Boston Liberal Arts/Medical Program

5)   GW BA/MD program

It's now early-November and you're just starting on these 5 apps (ideally you should've started them earlier). Since you were very busy with your November 1 apps in September and October, you haven't had any time to work on them until now. So, starting with your Drexel application, you work as hard as you can for the next month. When December 1 finally arrives, you realize that you've only had time to finish and submit the first 4 of them. Fortunately, the 5th program, GW, is a low-priority school for you, so you aren't *too* disappointed about not having the opportunity to apply. At least you were able to complete the apps for the schools that were more important to you.

Step 3: Get working on your apps!

No later than early September – around when your senior year starts – you should begin filling out your apps. Simply pick the one with the earliest deadline, and work on it – *just* that one – from beginning to end. This will probably be your most challenging app, since you'll have to create every essay and short answer from scratch. However, after finishing and submitting this one, you'll definitely have at least your "Why medicine?" essay all written up, making your subsequent apps a bit easier. Now begin working on the rest in groups of common deadlines (i.e., finish all the November 1 apps first, then the December 1 apps, etc.).

Be sure to save all drafts of all of your essays throughout the process, and reuse them for different apps whenever possible. For example, the "Why medicine?" prompt will almost certainly appear on each and every one of your GMed apps – don't hesitate to use the same essay for every app. But feel free to fine-tune the essay and make slight modifications based on each program's requirements and expectations as you see fit. Remember, it's okay to reuse your own essays for different apps – if you don't, you'll be working much harder than you need to be!

Conclusion

With this 3-step procedure, you won't have to waste time getting organized or taking care of mindless tasks *while* writing your essays. In the next chapter, we'll take a closer look at Step 3 of this procedure: you'll learn everything you need to write killer essays, become a savvy interviewee, and handle every other component of the application process with skill and speed.

Summary

- Before moving on, do the following:

  - Set up a Common App account.
  - Download all of the apps that you plan on submitting, and get a feeling for the difficulty of each one.
  - On a calendar, make note of all deadlines (and any other important dates) for every GMed program and normal undergraduate program that you plan on applying to.

- Here's a solid strategy for getting your apps organized and managing all of your work:

  - First, send out official transcripts and SAT/SAT Subject Test/ACT score reports to all of your schools.
  - Prioritize the apps with deadlines that fall on or around the same day based on their importance to you. Be sure to list 1-2 "safe" GMed programs on top, though.
  - No later than the first or second week of senior year, start working on the app with the earliest deadline.
  - After submitting your first app, start working on the apps in your prioritized list for the next upcoming deadline.
  - Reuse your essays as often as possible!

CHAPTER 11

The written application

I BET I know how you're feeling right now. It's sort of an uneasy, anxious, frustrated feeling – the same kind you get when you're made to sit through an advertisement on YouTube.

Don't you just hate those YouTube ads? They somehow manage to ruin just about every video you could ever want to watch. You could be just moments away from viewing Beyonce's new hit music video, headphones on, brimming with anticipation, ready for her voice to fill your ears and her image to fill the screen, when . . . an old man's voice catches you by surprise, and you realize that, before you get to hear anything about "single ladies" or "halos," you first have to listen to him tell you how Dulcolax® laxatives makes it easier for him to . . . you know. (Or worse, you could be forced to sit through an ad for the season premiere of *Grey's Anatomy.*) What a downer.

It's Ok if GMed apps get you down the same way – frustration is a completely natural response to such a massive workload. And as if drafting dozens of essays isn't hard enough, you also have to worry about sending transcripts to all the right places, making sure your teachers submit their recs on time, reading the longest chapter in this book, and staying organized and efficient the whole time. When you think about having to juggle all that *and* schoolwork for several months, it can be pretty discouraging.

But the best part of both YouTube ads and the application season is that, no matter how painful they are, they don't last forever. After a mere 15 seconds of unpleasant thoughts involving old men going to the bathroom, you're free to listen to Beyonce scream for however many hours you wish. Likewise, application season is just a few months of hard work; when it's finally over, you'll have years – literally, *years* – to relax, de-stress, and *not* worry about med school apps in college as a reward. So power through this YouTube ad we call "the application season" with me, because at the other end, there's one hell of a music video waiting for you.

Letters of recommendation

By now you should have about 2-3 teachers and 1-2 non-teachers who have agreed to write college recs for you. *(Taken by surprise? Check out Chapter 5 for tips on whom you should've asked for recs by now.)*

Now would be a good time to go through the list of required recs for each of your apps to make sure you've got them covered. If, for example, you realize that one of your programs asks for a rec from a foreign language teacher – and you haven't asked a foreign language teacher yet – *asking him/her should be your #1 priority right now.*

So, in this section, I'll be going over:

- How to ask for recs just a month or so before the application deadline,
- What to do for all of your teacher and non-teacher recommenders before they start writing your recs, and
- Which recs to send and where to send them.

Asking for one or more recs at the last minute

If you're over a month into senior year and you have yet to ask one or more teachers/non-teachers if they'd be willing to write recs for you, you need to make sure this gets done ASAP. Think about the experiences you've had with your sophomore, junior, and senior year English and science teachers – pick the ones with whom you've showed exceptional commitment, effort, and interest, both inside the classroom and through extracurriculars. You should aim to have 1-2 science teachers and 1 English teacher. Also be sure to pick 1-2 non-teachers – volunteer coordinators, doctors whom you've shadowed, or research mentors – whom you've worked with closely over the past few years. Additionally, if there are any oddball requirements from your apps (like the foreign language teacher example above), *be sure to ask those teachers as well.*

When you ask them if they'd be willing to write a college rec for you, be sure to:

1) Ask them *in person*,
2) Apologize for notifying them late in the game,
3) Offer a reasonable explanation for why your notification is late, and
4) Follow all of that up with a nice thank you e-mail, reiterating your apology and explanation.

What to do after you've asked (your teacher, that is)

After you ask that special someone out to prom, you don't just say, "okay cool, see you at the dance then!", turn around, and walk away. No – you follow it up with flowers, a dinner, and lots of other cutesy stuff. Same goes for the people writing your college recs . . . except not quite as cutesy.

Once you've asked your select group of teachers and non-teachers to write your recs (and they've said "yes"), you've got to follow it up with materials that'll make their job as easy as possible – and, in turn, will make your rec as awesome as possible. Before they write that one-page letter for you, provide them with:

- A copy of your resume.
- A written list of all the exemplary things you did in their class or on the job beyond just good grades and class participation. Reminding them of specific anecdotes or examples of your exemplary behavior (so they can mention it in their letter) will really help them write a solid rec.
- Make sure they know that you are passionate about medicine, either by 1) mentioning (and substantiating) it on the written list described above, or 2) by talking to them in person about it.

Now their job is to write you a 1-page letter of recommendation, preferably on school/employer letterhead. If they're really nice, they'll write 2 separate recs for you: one for your GMed programs (which will stress your passion for medicine and how you have the qualities of a good doctor), and the other for your regular undergraduate programs (which will focus more on your general strengths, personality, and work ethic, and perhaps briefly discuss your passion for medicine). If – and this is the much more likely case – they only write 1 rec (which you'll end up sending to both GMed programs and regular undergrad programs), no problem – *just make sure they know to talk about both your passion for medicine as well as some of your other exemplary traits and accomplishments.*

The bottom line is this: you want to have as much control over what goes into your rec without actually reading/writing it (because that's against the rules). So what do you do? You 1) provide your teachers and non-teachers with materials like your resume to guide them along, and 2) communicate with them as much as possible to make sure they understand your goals, interests, and ambitions.

After they've written your recs

Even after each one of your recommenders has written his or her 1-page letter, you're still not done – now comes all of the paperwork.

For most colleges, that 1-page letter isn't enough – they also want to see some forms come along with it. The most commonly requested form is the Common App teacher rec form: it's a quick 2-page document that asks for the name, address, phone number, etc. of you and your recommender, and includes a short checklist that asks your recommender to evaluate your personality. Schools that don't want the Common App teacher rec form will ask for a college-specific rec form, which is usually very similar to the Common App form. *All of these requirements and papers can get really confusing for your recommenders, so make sure you make their job as easy as possible.* Here's what you'll do for every one of your recommenders:

1) Take a look at the requirements for each of the schools you're applying to. Do they want the Common App rec form? A college-specific rec form? Download all necessary forms for each school.

   a. Fill out the dirty work on every form – your name, your address, their name, their address, etc. – so they don't have to.

   b. Check the box that says "I waive my right to access this recommendation" or something along those lines. Waiving your right makes your rec much more credible because it means you haven't seen it yet. When admissions officers know that your recommenders wrote it without you around, they pay more attention to what it has to say about you.

2) Give each recommender a packet that includes: the right number of copies of each rec form, and the right number of fully addressed/stamped envelopes.

3) Make sure they know what to do. If you think it'll help, give them a brief list of instructions. In most cases, once they've written their 1-page letter, all they need to do for each rec is: 1) fill out any remaining information on the rec form, 2) put both the form and the letter into the correct pre-addressed/stamped envelope, and 3) drop it in the mailbox.

Be sure to keep in touch with your recommenders as deadlines approach. *Politely remind them to mail each rec out at least a few days before the application deadline, and ask them to postmark the envelope if the deadline is only a couple of days away.*

Also – and this is very important – a few days after your recs have been mailed, call each admissions office to make sure they've received them. The last thing you want is for your chances of admission to be ruined just because one of your recs got lost in the mail.

Which recs to send . . . and where to send them

By now you should have about 4 different recs from a mix of teachers and non-teachers. But you won't be sending all 4 to every school you apply to – most will only ask for 2-3. So how do you know which ones to pick? Here's the deal:

Obviously, you should first make sure that you send all the required recs – so if a GMed program asks for recs from an English teacher and a science teacher, for heaven's sake, mail those two out already.

But it doesn't end there. Although it's not explicitly stated anywhere, you're more than free to send more recs once you've sent in the required ones. So if you have any recs that you really think are stellar (but aren't required by the school you're applying to), go ahead and send them in. Although these supplementary recs may not be considered as heavily as the required portions of your application, they still might help.

Consider the following scenario: you have recs A, B, C, and D. One of the GMed programs you're applying to asks for recs B and C, so you send those in. You're pretty sure that rec A is really good (because it was written by a teacher or non-teacher that really admires you), and rec D is just average. In this case, you should also send in rec A as a supplementary rec (don't waste your time sending rec D in). If the admissions counselors end up reading rec A, great – if not, sending it in definitely didn't hurt you.

Finally, just a quick warning: avoid sending too many supplementary recs. Send in 1-2 and you're providing extra helpful information. Send in any more and you're just spamming them; no matter how good they are, they'll just end up irritating the admissions officers. So as far as supplementary recs go, 1 is fine, 2 is fine, and of course, 0 is perfectly fine as well.

Summary

- Double-check that the people you've asked for recs meet the requirements for all the programs you plan on applying to. If all of a sudden you realize that you need, say, a rec from a foreign language teacher for one application, ask that teacher ASAP.

  - Remember to apologize to the teacher or non-teacher for the late notification, and offer a reasonable explanation for why your request for a rec is late in the game.

- After you've asked all the right people for recs, give them whatever they need to help them write the best rec possible. Provide them with: 1) a copy of your resume, 2) a written list of reminders, examples, and anecdotes of your exemplary behavior (hopefully ones that they'll be able to use in the rec), and 3) evidence that you are passionate about medicine.
- After they've each written a 1-page rec for you: 1) give them all the proper rec forms (with all the dirty work – like name, address, etc. – already filled out), 2) waive your right to access their letters, 3) properly addressed and stamped envelopes, and, if need be, 3) a brief list of instructions explaining what they should put in the envelopes before mailing them out.

  - A few days after all of your recs have been mailed, call each admissions office to ensure that they arrived on time.

- Although there's no need to send all 4-5 of your recs to every college, be sure to send: 1) the mandatory ones, and, if you wish, 2) 1-2 supplementary recs – but only if you're pretty sure that they say some really great things about you.

The resume: Putting it all together

Under normal circumstances, after spending nearly 4 years trying to finish something, you'd probably think that you were done and wouldn't ever have to worry about it again. Well in case you haven't noticed, we're not in Kansas anymore, Toto – this is the application season, where all forms of insanity and wickedness are fair game. That's right: even though you've been building your resume since freshman year, it's still not finished yet. But now, instead of *building* it, you'll have to worry about *putting it together*. That's why, in this section, I'll be talking about:

- What your resume should look like: organization, presentation, content, and wording.
- What an ideal resume looks like.

How you present your resume – what it looks like and how it's formatted – is almost as important as the actual content. It determines how well the reader recalls the important items on it, if he/she gets a solid overall picture of your interests, strengths, and abilities, and even if the reader thinks highly of you or not. No matter how stellar the content, it's possible for a disorganized resume – one that is unable to convey a clear message in a matter of seconds – to diminish the "wow factor" of the applicant's accomplishments.

On the next few pages, I've created an "ideal resume" of sorts – a sample resume with great content and great presentation. Analyze it closely, observe how and where key information is placed, make note of any important organizational features, and keep them in mind as you design your own resume. Afterwards, I'll highlight the most important characteristics of this sample. Note that, for the purposes of college admission, it's ok to have a multi-page resume – in the *real world*, though, you've gotta keep it to 1 page.

As you begin to read it, you may notice that this resume is, quite frankly, spectacular. It ended up becoming really extensive because, while I was writing it, I decided to include lots of examples of awards and activities that look good on a GMed application. So, although you should aim to make yours as presentable as this, don't be discouraged if it doesn't have as many items.

(Note: Almost all of the names, places, and institutions in this resume are purely fictional, as you might come to realize if you paid attention in English class.)

1234 West Egg Blvd.   Email: nick@greatgatsby.com
Long Island, NY 11030   Phone: (516) 555-1234

Nicholas Carraway

Education

1907-1911

West Egg High School

- Weighted GPA: 4.4
- Unweighted GPA: 3.9
- Class rank: Top 5%
- Completed 9 AP courses including AP Biology, AP Chemistry, and AP Calculus BC
- Ranked in the 99th percentile on the SAT (2320 out of 2400)

Professional
Medical Research

1909-1911

2 Medical Publications

- First author of a paper published in the *Journal of Awesome Medicine*
- Second author of a paper published in the *Amazing Medical Research Journal*
- Both projects conducted at the New York Center for Medical Research

March 1910

USASCMR National Medical Conference

- Submitted the 2 papers above to USASCMR (the United States Academy of Super-Cool Medical Research) review committee in September 1909
- Presented both projects to doctors and medical research from all 50 states
- Featured in an article in the USASCMR Annual Newsletter for work at the 1910 USASCMR medical conference

Summer 1909

Medical Research Internship

- Interned for 2 months at the New York Center for Medical Research
- Worked under Dr. Daisy Buchanan in the Radiology Research Department
- Conducted 2 medical research projects: The Effects of CAT Scans on Your Cat, and The Effects of PET Scans on Your Pet

February-April 1910

Science Fair Award Winner

- Used CAT Scan project from Summer 1909 medical research internship as science fair entry
- 1st place in the Medicine and Heath category at West Egg High School Fair
- 1st place in the Medicine and Health category at West Egg County Fair
- 3rd place in the Medicine and Health category at New York State Fair

Summer 1910

East Egg Medical Center Internship

- Interned for 2 months at the East Egg Medical Center
- Worked under Dr. Jay Gatsby in the Oncology Department
- Conducted 1 medical research project: The Effects of Cancer on Your Health

Academic Recognition	1908 **DuPont Challenge Award Winner** • Submitted an essay entitled, *Grasshoppers: A Threat to the Human Race?* to this national scientific essay competition • Winner of the $200 Honorable Mention prize • Chosen as one of the 27 award winners out of nearly 10,000 entrants in the U.S. that year 1910 **American Mathematics Competition Top Scorer** • Took the AMC 12 in junior year and placed among the top 5% of all students in the nation who took the exam in 1910 • Qualified for the AIME (American Invitational Mathematics Examination) September 1910 **West Egg Medical Center Scholarship Winner** • Selected for this $5,000 award based on active involvement in community service and an essay on the merits of volunteerism. September 1910 **College Board AP Scholar with Distinction Award** • Based on number of AP-level courses taken and high exam scores 1909-1911 **Honor Societies** • Member of National Honor Society • Member of French Honor Society
Patient Care Experience	1907-1911 **Local Free Clinic Volunteer** • Volunteer for West Egg Free Clinic twice weekly • Administer blood pressure tests to low-income, uninsured patients and refer those with hypertension to physicians at the clinic 1908-1911 **Urgent Care Center Volunteer** • Perform routine urgent care nurse activities at West Egg Urgent Care Center once weekly • Call patients and take vitals (temperature, pulse, etc.) • Also shadow various physicians and nurse practitioners at the facility April-May 1910 **Shadow Position with an Orthopedic Surgeon** • Shadowed Dr. Jordan Baker for 2 months at East Egg Hospital • Sat in on both patient-doctor conferences in an office and surgical procedures in an operating theater

Community **Volunteering**	1909-1911 **Founder of Elementary School Chess Tutoring Program** <ul><li>Founder of weekly after-school chess tutoring club</li><li>Teach young children at 3 local elementary schools how to play chess, foster competition among proficient young chess players, and encourage them to participate in local chess tournaments</li></ul> 1909-1911 **West Egg Assisted Living Home Volunteer** <ul><li>Assist elderly and mentally challenged residents with day-to-day activities and interact with them in social settings</li><li>Responsibilities include: reading books aloud, playing the violin, and organizing games</li></ul> 1907-1909 **East Egg Homeless Shelter Volunteer** <ul><li>Volunteered twice weekly</li><li>Activities included: preparing and serving meals and distributing proceeds and donations from local charities</li></ul>
School and **Community** **Leadership**	1909-1911 **Leadership Positions** <ul><li>Co-Captain of the West Egg High School Chess Team (1910-1911)</li><li>Founder of Elementary School Chess Tutoring Program (1909-1911)</li><li>President of West Egg High School Neuroscience Society (1909-1911)</li></ul> 1907-1911 **University-level Violinist** <ul><li>First chair of the first violin section in the West Egg High School Orchestra</li><li>Play in the first violin section of the West Egg University Orchestra following an audition in October 1908</li></ul> 1907-1911 **Model United Nations** <ul><li>Attend several local Model UN conferences every year, and have won 4 Gavel awards since freshman year</li><li>Won "Outstanding Delegation" award at 1909 West Egg University National Conference</li><li>Won honorable mention award at 1910 East Egg University National Conference</li></ul>
Interests and **Avocations**	<ul><li>Played JV Lacrosse during freshman year</li><li>Member of the Homecoming Theme committee during sophomore and junior years</li><li>Avid reader of Michael Crichton's works – have read 20 of his 30 books to date</li></ul>

Organizational Notes

The ultimate goal of organizing your resume properly is to *make it easy to both skim quickly and read slowly.* That is, a reader who takes a 1 minute glance at the document should be able to tell what your overall strengths, interests, and most important accomplishments are, while someone who reads every word of it should be able to 1) make it through without getting bored, and 2) recall almost every item later on.

This sample resume does a great job of making sure that both types of readers – the skimmers and the slow ones – get the most out of it. If you want yours to do the same, here are some important things you need to do to your resume:

- **Keep it succinct:** Every description, label, and title on your resume should be descriptive yet concise – you do *not* want anything to be too wordy. A good way to keep that from happening is to make the document highly structured. Nick Carraway's resume has a simple, effective structure that uses category headers (like "Professional Medical Research"), item headers within those categories (like "2 Medical Publications"), and bulleted descriptions of each item (because *no one* has the patience to read full sentences anymore). The use of different font sizes for each type of header makes the document even easier to follow.

- **Categorize your items:** Simply listing your awards and activities in no particular order might be a bit disorienting for your reader. Instead, separate your items into *clearly labeled categories.* Each category title gives meaning to the items under it. For example, someone who reads this sample resume will likely think of the "Urgent Care Center Volunteering" as a form of "Patient Care Experience," but the "East Egg Homeless Shelter Volunteering" as a sign of the applicant's dedication to the community. Collectively, these categories make the document very easy to skim, because they summarize the applicant's talents and abilities. For example, the sample shows that the student's strengths and interests lie in "research," "academics," "patient care," "community volunteering," and "leadership."

- **Use the best terminology:** In a document that boils the past 4 years of your life down to a few pages, word choice is incredibly important. Every word you place in the category headers, item headers, and bulleted summaries should predispose the reader to think about each activity and award in a certain way. For example, I could've titled the 2nd and 4th categories of Carraway's resume as "Research" and "Volunteering," but instead used "Professional Medical Research" and "Patient Care

Experience" to help the reader recognize the significance and medical nature of these experiences. This advice works well for non-medical items, too – word choice ultimately determines whether or not each item comes across as something sensational.

- **Put your items in the proper order:** This should be pretty obvious: items listed first on your resume are likely to receive more attention than those that are listed last. So *definitely mention your "big project" on the first page of your resume* and be sure to *place the most important item in each category at the top of that group.* The order in which your medical and non-medical categories are presented shouldn't be an issue as long as your "big project" comes first and your medical volunteering activities aren't dead last.
- **If necessary, write an objective:** At the top of resumes you often find a "goal" or "objective": a one-sentence summary of the person's skills and what he or she wishes to do with them in the near future. The purpose of that sentence is to unify every item under one common theme. It's up to you to decide if you need one or not – if you don't think your resume as a whole conveys one clear message, put one in. A possible objective for Carraway's resume might be: "To further explore the research and clinical realms of medicine while developing my interests in chess, the violin, and international affairs." I chose not to include an objective in the sample because I thought that the well-organized items and descriptive category headers clearly communicate the applicant's general interests and strengths. In the end, though, it won't make too big of a difference if your resume has one or not.

Content Notes

As critical as properly presenting your resume may be, it's also important to recognize solid accomplishments when you see them. Here are some things that make the *content* of Carraway's resume impressive:

- The duration of each activity shows commitment. The applicant held every volunteer position and extracurricular activity for at least 1 year and continued many of them all the way up through the year of his graduation.
- There's a good mix of medical and non-medical items. Through his extensive research, shadowing, and medical volunteering, this guy makes a pretty convincing case for his interest in medicine. But he's not one-dimensional: he's also interested in math, chess, the violin, Model UN, and community service.

- Every component of our Master Resume Template *(from the beginning of Unit I)* is included. Here's the breakdown:

  "Big project": The "big project" is on the first page and consists of the first 4 items in the "Professional Medical Research" category. This guy chose to do a research-oriented "big project" and took it pretty far: he not only published 2 projects from his first summer internship, but also presented them at a national medical conference and used them to win some pretty big awards at the science fair.

  Smaller medical activities: The research internship at East Egg Medical Center plus the volunteering and shadowing listed under the "Patient Care Experience" category make up this applicant's small medical activities.

  Non-medical experiences: This guy's got tons of them. He's the co-captain of his school's chess team; he's also a pretty sick violinist and an award-winning member of his school's Model UN group. What's more, he volunteers in non-medical settings like homeless shelters, assisted living homes, and elementary schools.

  Leadership: He's got this area covered pretty well, too: he leads his school's chess team and neuroscience interest group, and even founded his own chess tutoring club.

With a nice mix of all kinds of experiences, demonstrated commitment to each of them, and a clean, user-friendly presentation, this resume is a great example of what both GMed and undergraduate admissions officers would love to see.

Summary

- Study Nick Carraway's sample resume closely, paying special attention to key content and organizational features. While putting your resume together, keep these important elements in mind.
- To make your resume as clear and comprehensible as possible, 1) keep it succinct, 2) categorize your items, 3) use the best terminology, 4) put your items in the proper order, and 5) write an objective, if necessary.
- The content of Nick Carraway's resume is impressive because of the following features: every component of the Master Resume Template is included, there's a good mix of medical and non-medical items, and the duration of each activity shows commitment.

The essays

Introduction

A scientific poll that I recently conducted revealed that 99% of the adults in my neighborhood would rather have their mother-in-law over for the weekend than write another college essay (note that this poll has a ±1% margin of error). Yeah, they really suck that badly. This section won't reduce their suckiness, but it *will* help you 1) cut down the amount of time you spend on writing them, and 2) come up with a really great final product.

In this section, we'll go into:

- How and when to prepare for writing college essays
- Common essay prompts that show up on GMed apps
- General advice for your essays
- Advice on essays for the undergraduate part of your GMed app
- Advice on essays for the medical part of your GMed app
- A couple of sample essays that worked

When to start

"When to start working on college essays" is one of those things that everyone has a different opinion on. Your mom might tell you to "get a head start, darling," and begin writing at the end of junior year, while your (genius) best friend who got into MIT last year tells you that he started his essays 15 minutes before the midnight application deadline.

In the end, it all depends on how fast of a writer and creative-idea-generator you are. If you're a fast writer but you're not so great at coming up with new and interesting topics, you should start outlining and drafting your essays at the beginning of the summer between junior and senior year. As a warning, though, *do NOT start your essays any later than the beginning of senior year*, if you start any later, you probably won't have enough time to create quality pieces.

What to get

Before crafting any essays on your own, go to the library and check out a few "College Essay" books – the ones with pages and pages of sample essays in them. Stick with books published by big, trusted names like *Barron's*, *Fiske*, and *The Princeton Review* (I especially recommend the first two); they usually have the largest number of sample college essays collected from kids that got into the Ivies and other great schools. Do the same for "Medical School Essay" books – check out 2-3 books filled with sample essays written by medical school applicants, because they have to answer many of the same essay prompts that you do. Make sure to pick up books from at least 2 different publishers, as the quality of essays sometimes varies a bit between these companies.

These books will come in handy because they're each loaded with dozens of types of essays, each conveying different ideas in different ways. Although there are a couple of sample essays at the end of this chapter, having tons of them at your disposal will really help out in the early stages of your essay, as you'll see.

Common essay prompts

Even though each GMed program is slightly different from the next, they all want to know the same things about their applicants. As a result, you'll find that most GMed applications ask many of the same questions, just in different words. Below are some essay prompt themes that you'll probably run into more than once. We'll talk about ways to tackle these prompts in the next section.

Prompts on the Common App and undergraduate supplements

The undergraduate parts of your applications don't exhibit too much consistency. Aside from the Common App essay – which can be about anything you want – the 1-2 essays on your undergraduate supplements can be pretty different from college to college. The 2 most common themes are: *"Why do you want to attend this school?"* and *"What will you contribute to our undergraduate community?"* But aside from those, it really varies. For example, Brown's undergrad essay prompt a few years ago was: *"French novelist Anatole France wrote: 'An education isn't how much you have committed to memory, or even how much you know. It's being able to differentiate between what you do know and what you don't.' What don't you know?"* Pretty random, huh.

Prompts on GMed supplements

The GMed part of your applications exhibit much more consistency. Most GMed supplements include one or more of the following prompts:

- *"Why are you interested in medicine?"* Some variant of this prompt is guaranteed to show up on 99.9% of your GMed apps. From here on out we will refer to it as the "Why medicine?" essay.
- *"Why do you want to be a part of this school's GMed program?"* This question is tricky – in one essay, you'll have to explain why you're interested in this university, GMed programs in general, and this university's particular GMed program.
- *"Describe the biggest adversity you've ever faced and how you overcame it."* This prompt, although not as common as the previous two, gives the school a

sense of your maturity. How well do you handle difficulties and setbacks when they're thrown your way?

- *"Describe an ethical dilemma you've faced and how you overcame it."* Ethics make up a huge part of medicine. So admissions committees want to make sure that, when ethics are called into play, you can take actions that are strong, fair, and informed. A standard essay for this prompt might be about what you did when you saw your friend cheating on a test in math class. A more creative essay might draw from your experiences while interning in a research lab, shadowing a doctor, or playing in a varsity soccer tournament.

Of course, you'll come across a number of other prompts as you work on your apps, but these are definitely the 4 most common ones.

General advice on your essays

Before we go into the specifics of how to handle each essay, let's go over some general advice on generating ideas, writing essays, and evaluating them.

Coming up with ideas

The first thing you should do is look at the list of important experiences you've been compiling over the past few years. *(Don't know what list I'm talking about? See Chapter 3.)* What event or anecdote in your life can you build your essay around in order to effectively answer the prompt? If that process isn't fruitful, go back to your college essay (and med school essay) "how-to" books from the library – this is where they become really helpful. Read as many sample essays from these books as you can, and then think about the ones you like. What do they do well? For example, do they do a good job of taking a seemingly ordinary event and turning it into something much more meaningful and elegant? How can you emulate that style?

Writing the essay

Once you've come up with your idea, don't start writing – first outline it carefully so that it's well-structured, you know what you'll be talking about at each point in the essay, and it fits within the word limit.

After the first draft of each *type* of essay (for example, the first draft of your *"why medicine?"* or *"biggest adversity"* essay) run it by a friend/family member/teacher or someone else whose writing skills you trust. Since *your* perception of your writing is probably very different from that of others', you're likely to get some good feedback from them. They shouldn't be looking for nitpicky things like missing periods and commas – instead, they should be telling you what they think of your topic, what sounds right and what doesn't, and other general things like that.

Reuse essays whenever possible and as much as possible; it saves time and ensures that you are submitting quality work to every institution you apply to. For example, reuse your *"why medicine?"* essay every time an app has that prompt. Also, feel free to reuse the same ideas for different prompts. For example, if the anecdote you wrote about in your "biggest adversity" essay might also work well for your "ethical dilemma" essay on a different app, copy the story from the first essay, portray it as an ethical problem rather than an adversity, and build around it so that it addresses the "ethical dilemma" prompt well.

As great as it feels to reuse an essay, avoid just blindly copying and pasting essays from one app into another. Instead, spend a little bit of time customizing your reusable essay to each college. For example, if an 8-year program asks, *"why are you interested in this program?"*, edit your reusable essay a bit to stress the importance of a full undergraduate experience. If a 6-year program has the same prompt, tweak your essay to emphasize your desire to immerse yourself in medicine as early as possible.

Essay sets

Each one of your apps will include a set of many essays: the Common App essay, 1 or 2 undergrad essays, and 1 or more GMed essays. It's important to make sure that no 2 essays in the same app overlap. Here's what I mean:

Sure, it would look pretty bad if 2 essays in the same app have the same text or tell the same stories – be sure to fix things like that. But also make sure that your essays don't all discuss the same *topic* – namely, your interest in medicine. Try to have each essay reveal something different about you, so together they paint an interesting, diverse picture of you.

Advice on your undergraduate essays

Your undergraduate essays are very important for *undergraduate* admission (your resume and these essays are usually the 2 biggest determinants of admission). However, they aren't normally considered for GMed admission; rather, the essays in the GMed supplement have a say in that decision. But undergrad essays are still pretty important: as you might recall from previous chapters, for some schools the undergraduate admissions committee has to approve you before you're even considered for the GMed program.

There are 2 types of undergrad essays: the Common App essay and the ones on your undergraduate supplements. Let's go over both in more detail.

The Common App essay

The Common App essay is the most predictable essay: it never has a specific topic, so you can pretty much write about whatever the heck you want. Treat is as an introduction – something that your application reader can use to get a general sense of who you are. Avoid limiting yourself to a very medicine-y topic so early on in your app. Instead, pick something from your handy list of life experiences that reveals something about your personality. For example, you could recount an interesting anecdote from an important nonmedical volunteer activity and use it to talk about your compassionate nature. *Whatever you choose to write about, keep it under 1,000 words (about 2 pages single-spaced). Any longer and it probably won't hold your reader's attention the whole way through.*

Undergraduate supplement essays

As I mentioned in the "Common essay prompts" section a few pages ago, prompts for undergraduate supplement essays are pretty unpredictable. The best way to figure out how to respond to these prompts is to do everything we talked about in the "General advice" section, like reading plenty of sample essays and drawing from your list of life experiences.

One somewhat common prompt you might come across is *"Why do you want to attend this school?"* You don't necessarily need a flashy story from your life to answer this question as long as you have a solid reason and solid evidence to back it up. A bad reason for wanting to attend would be, "because it's a really prestigious school," or "because it has a GMed program." A good reason would be something *unique* about the school's opportunities that you learned from a campus visit or from talking to an alumn, not just from browsing the website one night. Be sure to mention the names of specific seminars/programs/initiatives/groups that support your reasons for wanting to attend – readers love to see that you're interested enough in the school to know exactly what is offered.

Unfortunately, since readers like to see specificity in your response, this particular essay will be tough to reuse in other schools' apps.

Advice on your GMed essays

GMed essays play a critical role in earning you an invitation to the *on-campus GMed interview.* However, in terms of actual admission to the program, they're probably the 2nd or 3rd most important thing, behind interview performance and tied with your resume. The impression you leave your on-campus interviewer with is almost always the most important deciding factor because the interview is the best way for the admissions committee to get a first-hand, unfiltered understanding of you as a person . . . . But more on interviews later.

The typical GMed supplement contains at least the *"why medicine"* essay; it may include 1-2 additional essays. Although the prompts for these additional essays vary, they sometimes include the *"biggest adversity," "ethical dilemma,"* or *"why this GMed program?"* prompts.

Let's talk about these essays in more detail:

The "Why medicine?" essay

This essay is almost guaranteed to show up on every one of your GMed apps, usually with a 500-word limit. It's also the one essay that GMed admissions committees focus on the most since it offers the most insight into your passion for medicine – so you want to make sure that this essay turns out to be a quality piece of work.

Since this essay is so important, most of the guidance in this section will focus on it. But keep in mind that most of this advice can be easily used to make your other GMed essays better as well.

Deciding what to write about

Answering the question, "Why medicine?" can be tricky because 1) you might not be sure of what specific things in your life pushed you towards medicine, and 2) you have to balance what you want to say with what your reader in the admissions office wants to hear; many answers that you may like are actually not as good as you think. Let's go over the basics of good and bad ways to respond to this prompt.

Passion: Whatever you choose to write about, showing near-insane levels of passion is absolutely essential. Passion for medicine shows the admissions committee that you're serious about becoming a doctor and sticking with the program for the full 6, 7, or 8 years. Imagine how you'd describe the rush of euphoria and energy you'd feel if your team won the Superbowl (unless you're a Redskins fan, in which case, uh, try to think about something else) and use that passionate language to describe your love for medicine.

What it should be about: One great way to address the prompt is to center your essay on an interesting anecdote or event from any point in your life that furthered your interest in medicine. *Then, you should explain how it is representative of the many things in your life that have pushed you towards medicine.*

What it shouldn't be about: That last italicized sentence is really important. Did one earth-shattering event convince you to dedicate your life to medicine? Not likely. And admissions committees know that. So unless it's really true, and you can say it in a really compelling way, it's probably not a good idea to write an essay about the one day you realized that medicine is your calling.

In general, there are 3 different ways in which most students answer the "Why medicine?" prompt. There's the essay that totally dodges the question, the essay that attributes your commitment to medicine to 1 life-changing event, and the essay that uses a combination of events throughout your life to justify your interest in the field. One of those 3 types is more mature and credible than the others . . . let's see if you can figure out which.

Table 1: 3 ways to write a "Why medicine?" essay, along with my cynical commentary.

Type of essay	The "ever since I was a child" essay	The "1 pivotal event" essay	The "I'm mature and insightful" essay
Text you might find in this essay	"I've wanted to be a doctor ever since I was a little kid. Whenever my brother and I played *Guess Who?* as kids, I always wanted to be the doctor character."	"Ever since that one week in 9th grade when I shadowed Dr. Johnson the pediatrician, I've wanted to be a doctor and put smiles on kids' faces too."	"A combination of different exposures and events have helped me realize that I have a passion for medicine."
My cynical commentary	Wtf. That doesn't answer the question. *Why* medicine? *Why* have you wanted to be a doctor ever since you were young?	It's probably not a good idea to attribute your dedication to 1 pivotal event, unless you think that event is *really* unique and compelling.	This is the best type of essay. It's realistic and it leaves plenty of room for stories and further elaboration.

One last topic you should avoid bringing up: medical TV shows. You do not want to give your reader even the slightest reason to believe that *House, ER, Grey's Anatomy*, or a similar show helped you decide that medicine is right for you. Most GMed admissions officers have a (perhaps understandable) deep, bloodthirsty hatred for those shows because they overdo the glamour and suspense and don't accurately portray the jobs of physicians. So don't mention those shows, or else they'll think that you don't have a realistic idea of what it's like to be a doctor.

How to write about it

Once you have something good to write about, follow these 3 guidelines for a great essay. No matter what your topic, these tips will make your essay sound even better. You'll find good examples of how to follow these guidelines in the sample essays at the end of this chapter.

Use passionate language: I've already mentioned this once, but it's worth mentioning again. Your job is to convince the reader that you *love* medicine and have a good reason for doing so – so write with *passion*. Think about how you'd describe the most breathtaking, fantastic, all-consuming thing you've done in your life and use that language to explain how you feel about shadowing surgeons in the OR, volunteering with physicians at a local free clinic, doing medical research, or something like that.

Use metaphors and stories: Everyone who's responding to this prompt is guaranteed to be writing about the same damn thing: medicine. So how do you spice your essay up? Use metaphors and stories. Rather than just *saying* that you love medicine, *illustrate* it by telling a story about, say, an exciting part of your medical service project in South America. And even when it's hard to tell a story, you can spice up your writing with metaphors. For example, it might be hard to tell a story about a day in the lab. But if you write a paragraph about how the breakthroughs and let-downs of research are just as thrilling to you as the ups and downs of a roller coaster, you're all set.

Make the beginning rock: A killer essay almost always has a killer opening. Although not an absolute must for a great essay, it can only help if the first paragraph – or even better, the first sentence – knocks your reader's socks off (out of *interest*, not out of anger or offense).

I've seen essays that begin with a short, intriguing sentence that make readers do a double-take; these essays usually turn out to be fantastic because the reader 1) is hooked from the very beginning, and 2) will very easily be able to recall that essay because of the awesome first sentence.

Sample essays

Here are 2 great essays written by real (and very successful) GMed applicants. Both applicants got into the schools that they wrote these essays for. Although both essays include many of the tips we talked about in this chapter, neither of them are totally perfect. See the bottom of each essay for a summary of their strengths and weaknesses.

(Sample Essay 1: Rice University) The quality of Rice's academic life and the Residential College System are heavily influenced by the unique life experiences and cultural traditions each student brings. What perspective do you feel that you will contribute to life at Rice?

The most important lessons in life are the ones that are learned through mistakes.

"Just great," I grumbled. My mentor was gone, and I had been left alone to defend our project. I felt horribly out of place: in a sea of MDs and PhDs at this international medical conference, I was the only one whose nametag screamed "STUDENT INTERN" in big blue letters. As I stood there, I noticed an elderly Danish physician point his nose up to read my project on liposarcoma. It was clear that he despised the project with a passion; he disdainfully told me that he was irritated by my use of unconventional antibodies. We deliberated over the project for nearly an hour – well into the midday break. Over lunch, in an effort to convince him that my methodology was valid, I showed him the details of my project data. After only a short while his mind had clearly changed – he even said that he would try to corroborate my findings with a project of his own.

I walked away from the ordeal almost triumphantly: not only had I debated intelligently with a physician, but I had also convinced him that the results of my project were legitimate. But all of a sudden that victorious sensation vanished: I abruptly realized that all the documents I had shown him, all the papers I had photocopied for him contained the confidential medical information of hundreds of cancer patients. I had left with him the complete medical histories of nearly every patient I had used in my project. As my throat sunk to my stomach, I did an about-face and hastily began searching the crowd for the man; maybe I could still find him. But he was nowhere to be seen.

Eventually, once my mentor returned, she and I were able to find him and reclaim our sensitive documents. Nonetheless, I couldn't shake my feeling of disgust for the way I had jeopardized the privacy of a hundred people. I had been so eager to argue with the physician that I didn't give even an ounce of thought to what I was showing him. Of course, my work at the international medical conference alone would be an experience worth sharing with my cohort at Rice. But ever since that incident, I've been more cautious, more thoughtful when I make decisions. To Rice I will bring a sort of scholarly diligence and patience that one can only acquire by learning from such a blunder. But fortunately, the unique qualities and life experiences that I will contribute do not all come from grim stories of failure and disappointment – I've had my fair share of lightheartedness, too.

"How is that *possible?*" the delegate from France exclaimed in disbelief at the paper I was holding at the front of the room. All the other delegates were dumbstruck, not sure whether to break into applause or laughter. The students in my Model UN committee had been toiling for hours, drafting resolution after incompetent resolution. In an attempt to promote nuclear transparency, they had written papers that referenced arcane, ambiguous clauses of ancient treaties. But the resolution I had just presented to the committee addressed no legislation; rather, it was based entirely on Boolean algebra. Who would've thought Boolean logic and truth tables could solve the nuclear crisis? My scandalous resolution arrayed overwhelming support and was quickly passed.

Two types of people attend Model UN conferences: those who love to get lost in endless debates over arms and drug trafficking and those who just want to build their résumé. But I am the third type of person. My goal at every conference is to catch people off-guard as often as I can – to propose as many outrageous ideas as possible. Over the past few years I've stimulated a number of committees lulled to sleep by emotionless argument: during one conference, I turned a dull speech into an impassioned poem. During another conference, I stirred up a flurry of excitement by dressing in pajamas to poke fun at the delegates who were sleeping in committee. For me and for those who recognize me at every conference, thrill and satisfaction always come from surprising others like this.

Many of my friends have come to depend on me for unconventional perspectives on issues both within and beyond the classroom. I am by no means simply a jester; instead, I am unique in the ways I approach arduous tasks. And it just so happens that my unorthodox thought process is often a source of pleasure, creativity, and humor for others. From just these two activities of mine – presentations at an international medical conference and Model UN – it is clear not only what exceptional life experiences I will contribute to Rice, but also what a contemplative, vigilant, and inventive personality I will bring. At Rice, I hope to offer to my cohort just as much as I receive from it; and what better way to contribute than to simply be someone with whom other students will want to cultivate their appreciation for knowledge.

Strengths:

• This essay includes lots of stories, which makes for a very interesting read.

- It uses energetic, descriptive language. Phrases like "pointed his nose up to read" and "despised the project with a passion" keep the essay interesting.
- There are no super-fancy words that seem forced or out-of-place, so the voice in the essay sounds very natural and relaxed.
- Although the writer does a good job of explaining his positive traits, it never sounds like he's bragging.

Weaknesses:

- The transition from the international conference story to the Model UN story is pretty confusing and unclear.
- In general, 2 stories is usually a little too much to squeeze into 1 piece of writing. Not only is it too much for the reader to follow, but it also makes the essay too long. This one is about 900 words total, which is extremely long as far as college essays go.
- It gets pretty melodramatic at times (Your "scandalous resolution?" Oh please. It's *Model UN* for crying out loud.)
- The beginning is alright. It's not super-catchy, but it's still interesting because it brings you right into the first story.

(Sample Essay 2: Brown University) French novelist Anatole France wrote: "An education isn't how much you have committed to memory, or even how much you know. It's being able to differentiate between what you do know and what you don't." What don't you know?

"Should we rat out a homeless man?"

As volunteers at a local free clinic, three of my friends and I can see from our desks a frail man step into a room at the end of the corridor, where hundreds of shopping bags are filled with clothing and canned food, one per patient. He emerges from the room holding five or six bags in his hands. *Thief!* I think to myself. But neither my friends nor I know what to do – report him? Keep quiet? After all, he's just like anybody else here – homeless. I secretly wish someone else will notice him and do something about it, just to relieve our burden – why are *we* the only ones to see him?

"Stop. He needs it."

Stop, my friends tell me. He needs all the sustenance he can get. But I'm not so sure. Of course he needs it – all of it – but at the expense of others? Six missing bags mean six famished children, six struggling families will leave the clinic only with a few carbon-copied health forms, but nothing to put in their mouths or over their backs. My friends will not rat him out, so the burden now lies only on my shoulders. Should I rat out a homeless guy?

"Uh-oh, he's leaving . . ."

It all happens too quickly. He glances furtively over his shoulder, bags in hand, and heads for the door. I jump to my feet, but am instantly paralyzed. *Sit back down!* I think. *No, chase after him!* My legs don't know what to do. I finally rush to the door, but he is nowhere to be seen. This week, he has escaped; this week, my friends win. It all happened too quickly.

"Excuse me, sir . . ."

Last week, he got away. But this week, I have to talk to him. I muster up the courage to walk over to where he sits. I speak to him quietly, so as to ensure that nobody learns of his deeds. I remind him softly that there are many other patients who need the food and clothing just as much as he does.

Let French Novelist Anatole France say what he pleases about education. The truth is: no amount of instruction will teach someone what to do in mind-torturing, split-second dilemmas. In hindsight, my decision to talk to the man neither pleases nor disappoints me; I still don't know what I should've done. Is his lifeless body laying bare and emaciated in some gutter because of what I did? Did anyone at the clinic benefit from the extra six bags I created? In a broader sense, is it better to take from the resources of many for the sake of one individual, or to sacrifice all of what one has for the greater good? For me, this quandary has transformed into a philosophical issue which is best summed up in one question, a question I will never know the answer to: should I rat out a homeless man?

Strengths:

- Not only does this essay respond to the prompt nicely, but it would also work well as an *"ethical dilemma"* essay.
- The unique format is fantastic – the italicized quotes that separate each paragraph make the sequence of events much clearer and make the essay appear much more fresh and captivating.
- It answers the question, "What don't you know?" in a very unique way. Instead of talking about academic knowledge, it calls attention to philosophical questions and personal integrity.

Weaknesses:

- It gets pretty melodramatic at times. Although phrases like "lifeless body laying bare and emaciated in some gutter" and "six famished children" are clearly used to make a statement, to some readers they may come across as over-the-top.

Summary

- Mothers-in-law are cooler than college essays. Now that's saying something.
- Start working on your essays during or before the beginning of senior year.
- Before writing your own essays, borrow some books from the library that contain tons of sample college essays and medical school essays.
- Common undergraduate essay prompts:

    - The Common App essay can be about anything you want.
    - *"Why do you want to attend this school?"*
    - *"What will you contribute to our undergraduate community?"*

- Common GMed essay prompts:

    - *"Why are you interested in medicine?"*
    - *"Why do you want to be a part of this school's GMed program?"*
    - *"Describe the biggest adversity you've ever faced and how you overcame it."*
    - *"Describe an ethical dilemma you've faced and how you overcame it."*

- General advice on essay-writing:

    - If you don't know what to write about, 1) consult your ongoing list of important life experiences, and 2) read lots of sample college and med school essays for inspiration.
    - When you finally sit down to write it, first 1) outline it closely, then 2) draft it, and 3) get feedback from people you know.
    - Reuse your essays as much as possible.
    - Every essay in an application should have different text, tell a different story, and reveal something different about you.

- Advice on undergraduate essays:

  - Avoid making the Common App essay too medicine-focused. Instead, write about something that reveals a bit about your personality.
  - If asked, *"Why do you want to attend this school?"*, your essay should mention something *unique* about the school's offerings and why that entices you. Mention specific names, groups, and programs at the university to show that you're *really* interested.

- Advice on GMed essays:

  - When answering the question, *"Why medicine?"*, use passionate language. Center your essay on an interesting anecdote or event from any point in your life that furthered your interest in medicine. Then explain how it is representative of the many things in your life that have pushed you towards medicine.

- How to write the essay:

  - Use passionate language.
  - Use metaphors and stories.
  - Make the beginning rock.

- Be sure to read the 2 sample essays at the end of this section and the critique that follows them.

Everything else on the written application

Ok great, so you've done pretty much all of the heavy lifting for the written application – your essays have been written, resume has been made, and letters of recommendation have been mailed. But even after you've done all that, there's a good chance your app still isn't complete yet – there are still probably some short-answer responses that need to be written, some silly little sections that need to be filled out, and – if there's any additional info you'd like to include along with your app – some mailing that needs to be done.

In this section I'll address such perennial questions as *"What the hell am I supposed to put in the 'additional comments' section if I have no additional comments?!"* and how to put other final touches on your app. Specifically, we're going to wrap up this chapter on the written application by talking about:

- How to deal with those pesky little sections on the Common App like the "Additional Information Section" and the "150-word short essay."
- What to do when the Common App (or any other application) asks you to summarize your resume into a frustratingly-tiny little chart.
- How to give your written application an extra kick with supplementary information.

Below are some sections that you might have some questions on even after writing your essays and filling out your basic info. These sections show up on the Common App and often appear on school-specific apps as well.

Additional Information section: This section of the Common App is very easy to fill: just upload a copy of your resume. Nowhere else on the Common App or on most undergraduate/GMed supplements is there any space for you to submit your complete resume. And of course, no matter how many of your accomplishments you reveal in your essays and elsewhere on your app, you want to be absolutely certain that a copy of your full resume gets into the hands of an admissions officer. So this is the perfect place to put it. Likewise, if you're filling out an application for a school that doesn't use the Common App, and you run into an "Additional Information" section, go ahead and stick your resume in there.

Listed accomplishments sections: On the Common App, this section is titled the "Extracurricular Activities and Work Experience" section. But this type of section also shows up on many undergraduate supplements and GMed supplements, and on virtually all application forms from schools that don't use the Common App. They're usually pretty frustrating since you're only given a small number of boxes (you almost always have more activities and accomplishments than there are boxes) and only 1-2 sentences' worth of room to elaborate on each activity.

It's important to make sure this list is as impressive as possible; although admissions officers aren't obligated to check out the resume you stuck in the "Additional Information" section, they are *definitely* going to look at the summary of your resume you made in *this* section. Here's what you should do:

While selecting items on your resume to put in this section, your objective should *not* be to just pick your most outstanding achievements. Since most, if not all, of the really sensational items on your resume are probably related to your "big project" *(see the "Resume" section in this chapter for more details)*, your list will look very one-dimensional if you just mention those. Instead, you should craft this section so that it conveys the same message as your actual resume: that you've explored a bunch of different fields, but are principally committed to medicine and/or helping other people. If you followed our Master Resume Template, you should devote: 1-2 items to your "big (research – or public service-related) project", 1-2 small medical activities (like patient care experience and volunteering), 1-2 non-medical activities (like chess, Model UN, a sport, or non-medical volunteering), and 1-2 awards or leadership positions.

Also, if you can manage to squeeze multiple, related items into one box, go for it. For example, if two items on your resume are about 1) publishing 2 medical research papers, and 2) presenting one of those papers at a conference, then try to mention both of them in one box on your list.

150-word short answer: This section of the Commonapp asks you to write 150 words (which amounts to about one big paragraph) on one of the extracurricular activities or work experiences from your list above.

It's important to make sure your 150-word short answer turns out well. For admissions officers, it can serve as a quick, easy-to-read reference on the quality and style of your writing; and of course, it's also a great way to learn more about one activity you particularly enjoy.

To clear up a common misconception, *the actual activity you write about is not incredibly important.* What matters is whether or not you can describe the experience creatively, and, above all, passionately. If you haven't mentioned your "big project" in any of your essays yet, then yes, this would be a great place to talk about it. But if you've already elaborated upon it in one of your essays, go ahead and pick something else on the list – anything – which you can tell specific stories about and write about passionately. In summary, write it the same way you'd write any other college essay.

Here's a good example of a 150-word essay that worked. It was written by a high school GMed applicant who founded a chess tutoring after-school club at her local elementary school. *(You may remember this example from the "Founding a Club" section of Chapter 3.)*

> The queen circles the king menacingly. A pawn is mercilessly killed. To me, chess is more than a simple board game; it is a thrilling medium through which two intellects can challenge each other. As a high school junior, I felt a desire to share my passion for the game with others – so I founded a school club. As the founder of the Elementary School Chess Tutoring Program, I persuaded a group of high school students to walk over to [my local] Elementary School with me every Monday to teach children how to play chess. The kids were thrilled when we teenagers watched them play; they soaked up every word of our advice. One week, when the session had been cancelled, I received an urgent e-mail from the coordinator at [my local elementary school], concernedly asking when we'd meet next. For my love for the club wasn't one-sided: everyone else enjoyed it too.

Supplementary information: There's a good chance that – after finishing your "big project" or any other accomplishment on your resume – there are some documents that you're really proud of. The classic example is this: after co-authoring a couple of medical research papers with your mentor, you have some pretty impressive publications on hand. Alternatively, if your "big project" was geared more towards public service, you may have an official portfolio of the work you did.

If you don't have any documents of this nature, no worries – sending supplementary information is entirely optional and not at all critical. But if you do have something impressive, go ahead and submit it along with your application! You can either:

1) Put it in the "Additional Information" section – if there *is* one – of one of your *undergrad or GMed supplements* (remember, the "Additional Information" section of the Common App is for your resume), or

2) Mail it to the admissions office in a manila envelope. Remember to put your identifying information on the document and to include a note requesting the recipient to add the document to your application file.

A good idea for the classic research example above would be to compile the titles, abstracts, and publication info for all the papers you co-authored into one document, and then send that in (*do not* send in any full-text papers). This document will 1) bring more attention to the fact that you've co-authored medical research papers, and 2) demonstrate your ability to work with complex medical concepts.

In the end, they may or may not look at this supplementary information; they already have several other materials from you as it is. If they read through it, great – it'll only call more attention to some of your significant achievements. But if they don't look at it, it won't help or hurt you at all.

Some important warnings, though: *do not send anything even slightly irrelevant, do not send anything excessively lengthy, and do not send too many different documents.* Any supplementary information you send should be no longer than 10 pages (just an abstract is good enough for any published papers), and should not consist of more than 2 different documents. Moreover, anything you send should be *very* pertinent to an item on your resume. Put simply, sending in too many things, excessively wordy things, or irrelevant things will not play in your favor – it might just end up irritating the person who reads your application.

Summary

- The "Additional Information" section in the Common App and in school-specific apps should be filled with your full, complete resume.

- For sections that ask you to list your accomplishments or summarize your resume:

  - Don't just pick your most outstanding achievements.
  - Pick a representative sample of activities and awards from your resume.
  - Devote 1-2 items to your "big project", 1-2 to your small medical activities, 1-2 to your nonmedical activities, and 1-2 to awards or leadership positions.

- The 150-word short answer section on the Common App is important because it serves as a quick sample of your writing.

  - Write about your "big project" if you haven't already done so.
  - Otherwise, it doesn't matter which activity you choose to write about so long as you write about it *passionately.*

- Only send supplementary information if it is *concise, relevant,* and *impressive,* and is closely related to an important item on your resume that you want to call attention to.

  - As an example, if you co-authored multiple research papers as a student intern, compile all the abstracts into one document and send it in.

CHAPTER 12

Interviews

I F ANY OF you guys have ever been on a date, you also know exactly what it feels like to sit through an interview. You could be sporting the most suave, dashing smile and calm, cool demeanor . . . but on the inside you just want to hide under the table, pee in your pants, cry in the corner, and do all sorts of other terribly unmanly things.

Sorry guys, but unfortunately, dates have always been, and will always be, like that. Interviews, however, don't have to be. With enough of an idea of what to expect, they can be remarkably simple. So, in this chapter, we'll go over the GMed interview essentials: what to say, what to know, and what to bring – as well as what your *interviewer* will say, know, and bring.

There are 2 different types of interviews that you will have to sit through: alumni interviews and GMed interviews. Chronologically speaking, alumni interviews usually come first – in the December-January timeframe – while the GMed interviews show up around February-March. Nonetheless, before you start your alumni interviews you should read this whole chapter, including the GMed interview section. Even though the 2 types of interviews are pretty different, an interview is still an interview – so the GMed section will definitely have some hints on how to handle your alumni interviewers.

Alumni interviews

The basics

The alumni interview is a normal part of any application for regular undergraduate admission. Typically, this is what happens: after you submit your application, an alumnus of that undergraduate school will contact you and ask to schedule an interview with you. After the interview, the alumnus will write a review – kind of like a letter of recommendation – describing their impression of you. They'll make note of your personality, your performance during the interview, and perhaps some of your important accomplishments. The alumnus sends the review in, an admissions officer adds it to your application file, and that's pretty much it. It's just another page in your application – just another perspective from which admissions officers can assess you. It's given just as much importance as any other item in your file.

How important are they?

For many undergraduate applications, the alumni interview portion is completely optional; admissions officers claim that it's just a different way of getting more information about you, and if you don't want to do it, that's totally fine. According to them, choosing *not* to have an alumni interview won't hurt your chances of admission.

The fact that it's optional probably gives you a good sense of how important it is to your application. Yeah . . . not very. As a part of your application for normal undergraduate acceptance, it's only of medium importance; as I mentioned earlier, it's given the same consideration as any other item in your file. Although it won't make or break your app (unless your interview goes absolutely dreadfully), it's still a nice way to show that you're personable student with good communication skills . . . . Which you are, aren't you?

As far as GMed programs go, alumni interviews are of even less importance. The alumni interview is just as important to an admissions officer as street signs are to a cab driver in Brooklyn. It's the on-campus *GMed interviews* that will really make or break your acceptance to these programs.

So . . . should I sign up for them? And when?

Even though these interviews are completely optional, it's still a good idea to do them for two reasons:

1) They show that you have a genuine interest in the undergraduate program and the school as a whole – not just the GMed program it offers.
2) They're an awesome way to practice and prepare for your GMed interviews.

Although not required, alumni interviews are a great way to show that you actually like the school you're applying to, and that you're not just applying because it has a GMed program. There's a chance that you might give, say, a Rice admissions officer the wrong impression if you apply to the MSP (Rice-Baylor's GMed program) but forgo the Rice alumni interview; it might seem like you don't give a rat's – er, donkey – about being an undergraduate student at Rice, and that all you care about is the GMed program. Also, even though they don't exactly replicate what you'll be facing during your GMed interviews, they're still great for honing your interviewing skills.

Most schools offer alumni interviews between January and March (although some schools let you schedule your alumni interview as early as October, even *before* you submit your app). *Try to schedule all of yours in and around January:* far enough from your GMed interviews so that you have time to identify and overcome any interviewing weaknesses you notice, but close enough so that all of this practice isn't long forgotten by then.

How to prepare

Schedule it at the right place: Just imagine what would happen if you had your interview at Chuck E. Cheese's or Hooters. It would be a disaster. First of all, asking your 50-something year-old interviewer to come down to a place like that is downright embarrassing and unprofessional. Secondly, both places are full of distractions: at Chuck E. Cheese's you have annoying little kids, and at Hooters you have . . . other things (um . . . distractingly-tasty buffalo wings?). That's why the location is really important. When your interviewer first contacts you, suggest a low-traffic coffee shop in the area (not a bustling Starbucks in the city – it'll probably be just as noisy as Chuck E. Cheese's), a bookstore, or a quiet deli/restaurant.

Know about the school: One question that I can almost guarantee your interviewer will ask is, *"Why do you want to attend this school?"* Even if you're genuinely interested in that school, it can be tough to formulate an intelligent answer on the spot – generic reasons like "everyone there is so nice," or "I really liked the atmosphere of the campus when I visited last month" won't cut it.

So the day before each interview, come up with a few specific examples of why you want to attend that particular school. Make sure to use anecdotes and observations you've gathered from college visits or any other interactions you've had with students, alumni, or faculty at that school. You can also use the school's website to find more material on unique curricular programs, the school's philosophy on education, and anything else that you think might help you answer the question more thoroughly.

But in general, even if you aren't asked that question, it's still a good idea to familiarize yourself with each school's unique qualities, programs, approach to education, etc. before your interview. The fact that you already know a lot about the university is definitely something that your interviewer will remember.

Play to your interviewer's interests: Your interview will go *so much more smoothly* if you talk about things that actually interest your interviewer. So the day before your interview, do a quick internet search on him/her. Nothing fancy – just type your interviewer's name into Google (or the search box on the university's website) and make a mental note of what pops up. If you find any meaningful info on the person – anything that you can relate to – try to devote at least a few minutes of your interview to that topic.

I remember this tip coming in really handy in one of my own alumni interviews: after a quick Google search the day before, I found out that my interviewer was an active member of the Lions Club (a community service organization with chapters all around the world). Although we ended up discussing all sorts of things during that interview, she became most engaged when I asked her about it. She really enjoyed talking about her experiences with the club and hearing about my own volunteer work. And above all, she was pleased to know that I had taken some time before the interview to learn more about her interests.

Remember that these are pretty inconsequential: Relax! Remember, as far as GMed admission goes, these interviews don't matter much; there's no need to super-over-prepare. Instead, it might do you some good to *under*-prepare: view these interviews as a chance to see how well you carry a conversation and answer questions on the spot, without too much prior thought. This will help you expose your weaknesses and hone your interview skills as the GMed interviews – the more important interviews – come around.

Read the GMed interview section: The second half of this chapter – which discusses the ins and outs of the GMed interviews – has some awesome tips that'll definitely help you out with the alumni interviews, too. Read it through, dude.

What to expect

What your interviewer will know about the school's GMed program: It completely depends on who your interviewer is. But more often than not, he or she won't know a whole lot – if anything at all – about the GMed program. Usually this is because the program didn't exist back when your interviewer was a student, or because (s)he was a non-science major and thus never really heard much about it. So make sure you know the ins and outs of the program, because there's a good chance you'll have to explain them.

What your interviewer will probably want to talk about: As you work your way through the interview season, you'll encounter 2 general types of interviewers: *standard* ones and *unorthodox* ones. Most, if not all, of your interviewers will be standard ones. They'll ask straightforward questions about your interests and accomplishments, like:

- Why do you want to attend this school?
- What are your interests and hobbies?
- What do you do in your free time?
- Elaborate upon one item in your resume.
- Do you have any questions for me?
- And plenty of other expected questions. Read the GMed interview section of this chapter for a longer list of common questions and ways to comprehensively answer each one of them.

And then there are the unorthodox interviewers. You probably won't run into these crazies any more than once or twice out of every 10 interviews. It's hard to prepare for these types of interviews because you can never tell when they're coming, and because they force you to improvise.

For whatever reason – perhaps because they think normal interview questions are boring and want to test your ability to engage in an impromptu, intelligent conversation – unorthodox interviewers choose to talk about the most random, unpredictable things. Things that are almost always unrelated to your resume or the school to which you're applying.

Here are some real-life examples of topics that college applicants have had to discuss with unorthodox interviewers:

- What are the differences between similar-sounding fields such as biochemistry, organic chemistry, and molecular biology?
- What was the biggest mistake of the 20th century? Why? Who committed it?
- Who bears the blame for the development of a child's bad habits or poor personality – the parent or the child?
- Which poses a greater threat to a given society: people with the intent to inflict harm upon others, or the weapons they use? (i.e. which is more dangerous: a gun or someone who wants to use that gun to hurt other people?)

As you can see, the interviewer is at liberty to discuss with you whatever the hell he or she wishes. And the hardest part is having to think up an interesting, thoughtful comment in response to each one your interviewer makes. Although you won't be able to prepare your responses in advance, here are some general pointers:

1) Many questions that an unorthodox interviewer might ask are dichotomous (consider the real-life examples above: parent or child? gun or gun-wielder?). That is, you'll have to pick one side or the other and substantiate your choice. If it just so happens that your opinion differs from your interviewer's, not a problem. Simply defend your position,

acknowledge the validity of your interviewer's position, and move on. Avoid just mindlessly acquiescing to your interviewer's opinion, but more importantly, *do NOT engage in a debate with even the slightest degree of hostility.*

2) It's ok to ask your interviewer discussion-provoking questions related to the topic at hand, too. In fact, it might even help make the conversation more interesting for him or her. Which is a good thing.

3) Stay on top of current events around the world during the interview season. News stories (and the background on those stories) are really great fodder for the analogies and comparisons you'll make and evidence you'll provide during your unorthodox interviews.

4) As always, read the GMed interview section of this chapter for more tips.

What to say

For any of the normal, predictable questions that your interviewer might ask, here are some guidelines on what your response should sound like:

What to say about medicine: As a general guide, try not to sound over-the-top passionate about medicine the same way you might during a GMed interview. To an alumni interviewer evaluating you for undergraduate admission, it's possible that such an unyielding commitment to one particular field may come across as a bit presumptuous. Typically, your American undergraduate years are considered a time for academic exploration and self-discovery. So sure, go ahead and talk about your passion for medicine and healing people; but also be sure to mention your wide array of other experiences and interests.

What to say about the school: In the "How to prepare" section a few pages ago, you came up with some specific examples of why you want to attend this particular school – be ready to whip that out when the time is right. *Do* let him or her know that you've applied to the GMed program, and that you're very interested in it. But also make it very clear that you're interested in the undergraduate school, too.

What to say about your resume: It totally depends on how much your interviewer knows about you already. As you'll learn in the upcoming GMed interview section, your interviews will either be *blind* or *non-blind.* In a blind interview, your interviewer knows absolutely nothing about you before the interview except for, perhaps, your name. In a non-blind interview, your interviewer already knows a bit about your interests and activities in advance (usually because the university forwards some info from your application – your resume, perhaps a short essay – to him or her). Your objective during a blind interview should be to familiarize your interviewer with all the important items on your resume.

During non-blind interviews, don't just reiterate what he or she already knows about your accomplishments. Instead, share *new* stories and *new* insights – things that don't show up on your resume or other application materials. For example, with a non-blind interviewer who already knows that you worked in a medical research lab last summer, you could share an interesting or funny story about something that you had to do as an intern there.

What to say about everything else: The key to making sure your interview goes well is to give your interviewer what he or she wants, and to leave out what he or she doesn't want. How do you tell the difference? *You gauge the interviewer's attitude.* Now I'm not gonna give you a 200-page psychoanalytic lesson on how to read a person's tone of voice and body language, but I will say that it's pretty easy to tell when someone is – or *isn't* – enjoying what they're hearing. For example, if you bring up the GMed program and your interviewer seems to be put off by such an early commitment to medicine (whether it's through facial expression, tone of voice, or something as obvious as a critical comment), steer clear of that topic for the rest of the interview! Instead, talk about the fields you'd like to explore as an undergraduate student – because if she doesn't like commitment, then she's sure to like academic exploration.

Note: This tip – about constantly gauging your interviewer's attitude – is one of the most important pieces of interview-related advice you'll ever get. *It shows that you shouldn't keep your responses to certain questions exactly the same for every interview, because every interviewer has different opinions and preferences.* The practice of gauging will help you adapt your responses so they are in line with what your interviewer favors the most.

What to say (and do) after the interview: At the end of the interview, give them a copy of your resume. No later than the day after the interview, send your interviewer a "thank you" e-mail. Make sure to include some specific, unique details about your interview in the e-mail to help them remember that it's *you* saying "thank you" and not one of their other interviewees. For example, part of your e-mail might say:

> Thank you very much for taking the time to sit down and talk with me yesterday. I really enjoyed discussing [something generic here, like 'the unique curricular offerings at Union College'], in particular, [something more specific here, like 'it's Scholarly Concentrations Program'].

. . . along with some more specific details to make it seem even more personalized. Citing what you guys talked about specifically will also show your interviewer that you enjoyed the interview enough to remember some key points from it. Also, if you forgot to give your interviewer a copy of your resume, attach it to this e-mail.

Summary

- An alumni interview is no more or less important than any other part of your written app. After the interview, your interviewer simply writes a page on your performance and includes it in your application file.
- They're usually optional, but you should still do them to 1) show your genuine interest in the school, and 2) practice for your GMed interviews. Schedule them for January.
- How to prepare for an alumni interview:

    - Schedule it in a professional, quiet place.
    - Know about the school beforehand.
    - Play to your interviewer's interests.
    - Remember that alumni interviews are pretty inconsequential so long as you don't bomb them.
    - Read the upcoming GMed interview section.

- What to expect during the interview:

    - Your interviewer might not know much about the school's GMed program, so be ready to explain it.
    - If you have a normal interviewer, they will likely ask you questions like: *Why do you want to attend this school?*, *What are your interests and hobbies?*, *What do you do in your free time?*, *Elaborate upon one item in your resume.*, and *Do you have any questions for me?*
    - If you have an unorthodox interviewer, there isn't much you can do to prepare. Just keep on top of the news and be ready to engage in an intelligent discussion.

- What to say about . . .

    - *Medicine:* Definitely express your interest in medicine. However, an insane display of passion is not necessary.
    - *The school:* Cite specific examples and/or anecdotes that justify your interest in the school.
    - *Your resume:* If the interviewer is *blind* (i.e., didn't read it beforehand), talk about the 3-4 most important things on your resume. If the interviewer is *non-blind* (i.e., already knows a bit about your accomplishments), share *new* stories and experiences.

- Constantly gauge your interviewer's attitude to figure out what they do and don't want to hear.
- Send a specific, personalized "thank you" email after the interview.

GMed interviews

After you've sent in all of your application materials, the next step is to tackle the on-campus GMed interviews. Being selected for GMed interviews is a pretty big deal: from a total applicant pool of a few thousand, the more popular GMed programs will invite about 100 students – or about 2 times as many students as they plan to admit to the program – for GMed interviews. From this pool, most programs extend offers of admission to 30-50 students, although some programs accept as many as 100 or as few as 6.

If a school you applied to likes your essays, resume, and the rest of your written application, they'll contact you around January or early February via phone, e-mail, or snail mail to invite you for an on-campus GMed interview. Usually they'll give you a few dates to choose from (some colleges don't give you an option, though); once you respond to them with your preference, you'll have to visit the campus that day for your interviews. That's right, *visit the campus*: so if you're invited to the University of Rochester's REMS interview and you live in California, you'd better book a flight to New York, baby. If droppin' all that cash on plane tickets has you bummed out, no worries: regular pre-med students have to do the same when they're applying to med schools, too. (. . . after taking the MCAT and building their resume, that is.)

Once you've been invited to a GMed interview, you're pretty much on a level playing field with all the other interviewees. The admissions committee certainly doesn't burn your written application after they've invited you – but the truth isn't far from that, either. *Your performance during these interviews is almost always the #1 determinant of whether or not you get into a program.* Sure, there's a good chance they'll look over your resume or essays again to help them come to a decision – but those are of secondary importance compared to the GMed interview. This is because there are some things – like personality, passion, and confidence – that you can only truly understand about a person by talking to them firsthand.

Since GMed interviews are so important, we're going to spend a lot of time talking about them. Here are the topics we'll be covering:

- Interview format
- Student interview tips
- Faculty interview tips
- Typical interview questions
- Answers to typical interview questions
- How to prepare for your GMed interviews
- Tips for all other parts of interview day

Interview format

GMed interviews are usually drawn out into all-day events in order to make sure that travelling all the way to the school is worth your while. On your interview day, you're likely to have a series of 30 min-1 hr interviews scheduled for you. Although each program does it a little differently, you'll probably have some combination of the following:

- 1 interview with a current med school student in that GMed program, and
- At least 1 – but no more than 2 – interview with a med school professor, administrative director of the program, or some other faculty member at the school.

The vast majority of these are normal, conversational, and 1-on-1. However, the occasional school will try to mess with you by conducting a panel interview (that is, an interview with 2 or more faculty members at the same time), or by asking you tricky questions during the interview. Tips on how to handle these are coming up later in the chapter.

The rest of your interview day will be filled with no-pressure activities like big group lunches with current GMed students and faculty, campus tours, and info sessions.

Types of interviews

Every interview you have will be either *blind* or *non-blind*. Although we briefly touched on this in the "Alumni interviews" section earlier in the chapter, it's especially important to know this for GMed interviews.

- *Blind interview*: In a blind interview, the interviewer knows nothing about your essays or resume beforehand (a.k.a., he was too lazy to read them). In this type of interview, try to familiarize your interviewer with the *important parts* of your resume so that, by the end of it, he's aware of your most significant accomplishments, credentials, and interests. This has to be done very carefully or it'll come across as bragging. Rather than force-fitting this info into the conversation, let it come up naturally. Also, don't worry about bringing up common stuff like National Merit or honor societies that you're a part of; instead, mention things that really show your interests and personality, like your "big project."
- *Non-blind interview*: In a non-blind interview, the interviewer has read your application materials and has at least *some* idea of your accomplishments in high school, what you wrote about in your GMed essays, etc. Don't expect them to have a perfect memory, though . . . after all, they've

probably read hundreds of GMed apps along with yours. In this type of interview, your goal is to show that you're more than just your resume. Share *new* stories and *new* compelling reasons behind your passion for medicine, while briefly referring back to a few of the biggest things on your resume to remind him of what you've achieved.

No one will ever *tell* you if your interview is going to be blind or non-blind. But don't worry: through their questions and comments, you'll be able to tell how much your interviewer already knows about you within the first few minutes of the interview.

Student interview tips

About half of all GMed programs throw in a student interview in addition to their 1-2 faculty interviews. The dynamic of an interview with a student (usually a med school student) is quite different from that of an interview with an adult. Let's go over ways to make sure that your student interviews go well.

The student interview is usually a *blind* interview and is often conducted by a sleepy and/or uninterested med student who really doesn't want to be doing this. In many cases, he'll be asking you a list of generic questions about your interests and personality given to him by the faculty.

Your job is to make him less bored. If you manage to keep your student interviewer amused and engaged, then you've done well – he'll definitely remember you for that. The best way to do this is to be *animated* when you speak: use exciting gestures and a lively voice to keep the conversation engaging.

As with any blind interview, be sure to mention the most important parts of your resume. This brings us to the first in our 2-part series of "things to watch out for" during your student interview.

- *Thing to watch out for #1:* The student's reaction to your accomplishments. Keep in mind that this student isn't too much older than you are, so his reaction might not be what you'd expect from an adult. Rather than being impressed, he might feel a bit intimidated. Make note of his reaction as you talk about an item on your resume. Does he seem genuinely impressed? Or does he quickly respond to your accomplishment with one of his own? If it's the former, feel free to elaborate a bit more. If it's the latter, be a little cautious. Reveal just enough about your achievements so that he knows you're a qualified candidate for the program, and then stop there.
- *Thing to watch out for #2:* Your interviewer's personality. You'll either get a student who's formal and uptight, or chill and laid-back. Your responsibility is to give him what he wants. If your guy is really chill, he probably won't appreciate it if you're stiff and distant the whole time. Likewise, if he's really

uptight, he probably expects you to be just as proper. As a fair warning, though: even if your interviewer is a total chillster, you should avoid using slang and absolutely *never* use curse words. You should maintain some level of professionalism at all times.

In general, the purpose of the student interview is to make sure that you can communicate well not only with adults, but also with people around your age. Relax during your student interviews – they're usually not as heavily weighted as your faculty interviews. But just blowing them off as unimportant raises a big red flag for the admissions committee and greatly decreases your chances of getting into the program.

One last piece of advice: most students *love* to talk about themselves. Give them what they want and ask them a couple of questions about themselves. You can ask them about anything – what they like about the program or the school, what they do with their time in college, what they did in high school, the list goes on. This gets them involved in the conversation and shows your genuine interest in the program.

Faculty interview tips

Faculty interviews are usually conducted by a med school professor or an administrative staff member of the GMed program. Faculty interviews can be blind or non-blind – you won't really be able to tell until after the first few minutes of the interview. For this type of interview, you want to come across as relaxed, pleasant, confident (but not *over*-confident), and professional.

When talking about your research or any other high-level medical project, you might feel like showing off some of your technical knowledge. Use that advanced medical terminology a bit when your interviewer is an M.D. – i.e., someone who will understand that stuff – to show that you're aware of and comfortable with some complex medical concepts. For interviews with administrative staff, though, stick to using simpler terms to explain your project. Technical detail that he or she doesn't understand will, in turn, make your explanation hard to understand.

Perhaps the 2 most important things you'll have to remember to do during every interview is 1) be passionate and 2) constantly gauge the interviewer's attitude.

- *Be passionate:* I said it a couple of times in Chapter 11 and I'm going to say it again: every GMed admissions officer out there is looking to accept people *passionate* about medicine and about the program. Through voice, body language, tone, excited expression, and detailed elaboration, make it sound like that medical project you did was the most exciting thing you've ever done and you could talk about it forever.

- *Constantly gauge your interviewer's mood*: Just as important as showing passion is telling your interviewer what he wants to hear. In order to understand what exactly he wants to hear, you'll have to figure out his opinion on the topic you're discussing with him, his mood at the time, his general demeanor, and things like that. *How?* It's nothing new – you do it all the time during conversations with friends, family, and everyone else. Just do it more carefully now. Pay attention to your interviewer's facial expressions, body language, tone, and language throughout the discussion, and respond accordingly. For example:

  - If he seems pretty worn out from conducting back-to-back interviews all day, kick your enthusiasm up a notch and try to engage him more.
  - If he seems turned off by your overzealous attitude and long-winded answers, assume a more down-to-earth tone and give more concise answers.
  - If he doesn't seem to agree with the "accelerated undergrad" portion of the program, stress the importance of the undergraduate experience and mention some non-medical subjects you'd like to explore as an undergrad.

You'll see tons of other examples of when you'll need to gauge your interviewer's mood in the "Typical interview questions" section coming up. It just goes to show that *answers to many common questions totally depend on what kind of person your interviewer is.*

A note on time limits

Most of your interviews will last somewhere between 30 min-1 hr. In some cases, if the conversation is really interesting, your interviewer might let it go on for a bit longer than that. But in most cases, your interviewer will have to cut the interview off at 30 min or 45 min because they have a fixed schedule of interviews that they have to get through that day. If your interview has a strict time limit like that, just be aware of it. Budget your time wisely so you can get all your important points in before time's up.

Typical GMed interview questions

Very common questions and discussion topics:

- Tell me about yourself.
- Why do you want to go into medicine?

- What role did your parents have in your decision to apply to GMed programs and pursue a career in medicine?
- Tell me about this one particular item/event I read about in your resume/essay.
- Why do you want to go to *this* school?, or Why do you want to be a part of *this* GMed program?
- Do you have any questions for me?

Less common, but not *un*common, questions:

- Do you know what specialty you want to go into after med school?
- Where do you see yourself in 10-20 years?
- What are your strengths and weaknesses?
- Describe a time when you faced an ethical dilemma. How did you handle it?

Answers to typical GMed interview questions

"Tell me about yourself."

Your interview will almost always begin this way. This is *not* the same as asking *"Why medicine?"*, so don't start by talking about medicine – that might make you come across as one-dimensional. Talk for a bit about who you are, where you're from, your interests and hobbies, and things that reveal your personality. Once you've given your interviewer a brief look at the other aspects of your life, you can slowly transition into how your passion for medicine developed.

"Why medicine?"

Yup. It's the same question that you had to write an entire essay on. But don't give your interviewer the same exact answer you gave in your essay, especially if it's a non-blind interview. Keep the *theme* the same, though. For example, if you said in your essay that you love medicine because you want to help people in developing countries, stick to that in your answer. But use new anecdotes and examples to explain it.

Sometimes the interviewer will try to test the integrity of your answer. For example, if you say something along the lines of, "I want to be a doctor because I want to relieve people of their suffering," there's a chance that he'll respond with:

> There are tons of professions out there that relieve people of suffering: social workers, personal injury lawyers, human rights workers,

paramedics, philanthropists, etc. Why medicine *specifically?* What's different about medicine that makes you want to pursue it as a career but not any of these other professions?

Be prepared for this question, because some of your interviewers will ask it.

"What role did your parents have in all of this?"

This question is pretty straightforward – they just want to make sure that going into medicine and applying to GMed programs are *your* decisions, not your parents'. Your answer to this question should reveal that your parents are mildly interested in your educational and career choices, but no more that that. Sure, they support you in your choices, but ever since the beginning it's been *your* decision to go to med school and *your* independent effort that has earned you all the medical experience on your resume. Feel free to use an example or some further explanation to make that point clear.

"Tell me about this one particular item on your resume."

This should be really easy for you. Just remember to show lots of passion as you describe the event or activity in detail and share some short anecdotes about it.

"Why this school?" or *"Why this GMed program?"*

Prepare yourself ahead of time for this question. Before your interview, do some research on the unique programs/opportunities/courses that the school offers, and use that to develop a compelling answer to this question. Your answer should be not only about the school, but also about how its offerings play to your strengths. In other words, don't explain why it's a great school – explain why it's a great school for *you.*

"Do you have any questions for me?"

Your interview will almost always end this way. Definitely ask some questions – it'll show that you're interested and well-read on the school. The day before, do some research on the school and prepare a couple of intelligent questions on its unique aspects. Also, bring a pad and pen so you can jot down quick notes while he's answering your questions. This is a great way to show that you're paying attention, you're interested, and you appreciate his advice.

A quick note on general knowledge and current issues

During interview season (late January-early March), it would be a good idea to read up on issues like abortion, euthanasia, stem cell research, and animal experimentation, because the occasional moron might ask you a question that requires you to pick a side on one of these issues and defend it intelligently. You'll also want to keep up with the news during the interview season – if current events ever come up in the conversation – which they occasionally do – showing that you know what's going on in the world is a huge plus.

How to prepare for your GMed interviews

Several days before the interview

Formulate and rehearse: Starting at least a week before your first interview, formulate your answers to all of the common interview questions in this chapter and rehearse your delivery of those answers all the way up until the actual interview.

When I say "formulate your answers," I mean jot down a few bullet points (or even better, just make a few mental notes) on how you'll respond to each question. *Do not* make a line-by-line script of what you'll say.

And when I say "rehearse," I mean practice clearly delivering these answers in front of a mirror, with friends or family, or alone in your room. *Do not* try to memorize any of your answers word-for-word. Remember, this is a conversation, and in a conversation, speeches 1) almost always sound forced, and 2) are really easy to mess up. Instead, just know the main points you want to cover in each answer, and practice covering those points in a conversational manner. Put simply, *rehearse sounding non-rehearsed.* Practice inserting pauses in your answer so you have time to think and put together your next sentence. Practice leaving wiggle room in your answers for impromptu digressions and elaborations. The less you make it sound like a Q&A firing session, the better.

After a few interviews at different schools, you won't have to spend nearly as much time on this since you'll already be comfortable with answering common questions and quickly coming up with material to answer unexpected questions.

The day before the interview

The day before, do the following:

- Prepare your business suit/outfit.
- Fill out and pack any paperwork that you were told to bring with you to the interview.
- Pack your photo ID.

- Pack a pad and pen so you can jot down useful notes during your interview.
- Turn off your cell phone so it doesn't distract you during the interview.
- Print off 2-3 copies of your resume to give to your interviewer(s) at the end.
- Do some online research on the school and its unique offerings. Then 1) incorporate this info into your answer to the question *"Why this school?"*, and 2) use the info to come up with a couple of specific, intelligent questions about the school or the program. Remember to ask these questions at the end.
- If you have the names of your interviewer(s) ahead of time, do a quick Google search on them. Aside from gauging your interviewer's mood, this is another great way to figure out what your interviewer wants to hear and likes to talk about. From your search you might learn about the kinds of papers he's published, organizations he's a part of, or things he likes to post on his blog or webpage. Briefly mentioning these things – and even expressing your interest in those areas, too – will not only flatter him (which is always a plus), but will also give him an opportunity to have a conversation with you on a topic that he genuinely enjoys discussing.
- *Don't freak out!* Remember, it's not a test, it's just a conversation. For 45 minutes. With a real doctor. Not to mention, the most important conversation of your life.
- Okay fine, maybe you can freak out *a little* – but don't let your nerves ruin your performance.

Tips for all other parts of interview day

- *In the waiting room with other students:* While you're waiting to be called for your interview, you'll probably be placed in a room with all the other candidates interviewing that day. Be cordial and open with them! Start a conversation if there isn't one going on already. It'll just give you a sense of who you're up against and get you in the right mood for your interview.
- *Between interviews:* If you're scheduled for multiple interviews that day, you'll probably return to that same waiting room. While you're there, talk to the other students. Ask them how their first interview went, who their interviewer was, etc. – you might learn a thing or two about your next interviewer's personality or interests. This is a *huge* advantage because you'll know what to expect before you even meet that interviewer.
- *Tours, info sessions, and lunches with GMed students and faculty:* Again, be cordial and conversational. Even though you're not being judged during these events, you still need to be on your best behavior. Ask a few intelligent questions to show your interest. If there are any faculty members at the event, make a special effort to talk to them. There's no need to be in their

faces at all times, but you should still make sure that they know who you are and that you're really interested in the program.

- *After the interview day:* Email an individualized "thank you" note to all of your interviewers and any other faculty members you may have spoken to that day. Keep the letter no more than a paragraph long and cite a couple of specific, positive things you both discussed during the interview so they remember who you are.

Once you've done all that, you're officially done with the entire application process! Woo! There's only one thing left to do: wait until late March-early April to hear back from the GMed admissions committee on their final decision!

Summary

- If the school likes your application, they'll contact you around January or early February to invite you for an on-campus GMed interview.
- Once you've been invited to a GMed interview, you're on a level playing field with all the other interviewees. Your performance during these interviews is almost always the #1 determinant of whether or not you get into a program.
- Your interview day will usually consist of:

    - 1 interview with a current med school student in that GMed program.
    - 1-2 interviews with a med school or GMed faculty member.

- There are 2 types of interviews:

    - *Blind:* In a blind interview, the interviewer knows nothing about your essays or resume beforehand.
    - *Non-blind:* In a non-blind interview, the interviewer has read your application materials beforehand.

- Student interview tips:

    - Student interviews are usually blind.
    - It'll usually take the form of a current med student asking you a list of generic questions given to him by the faculty.
    - Be animated when you speak to keep him engaged.
    - Don't push your credentials too hard if he reacts adversely to hearing about your accomplishments.
    - If he's being proper, be proper. If he's chill, be chill.

- Students love to talk about themselves – so ask him a question or two about himself.

• Faculty interview tips:

- Faculty interviews can be either blind or non-blind.
- Be passionate when you talk.
- Don't be discouraged by your interviewer's attitude. Instead, try to gauge his personality, mood, body language, and opinions throughout the interview and respond accordingly. If he seems really opinionated, avoid making any statements that he might feel the need to argue against. If he seems shifty, impatient, and inattentive, you should be more animated, pose questions for him (to get him involved in the conversation), and try not to drag the interview on for too long.
- Be aware of any time limits on the interview.

• Typical GMed interview questions and discussion topics:

- Tell me about yourself.
- Why do you want to go into medicine?
- What role did your parents have in your decision to apply to GMed programs and pursue a career in medicine?
- Tell me about this one particular item/event I read about in your resume/essay.
- Why do you want to go to *this* school? or Why do you want to be a part of *this* GMed program?
- Do you have any questions for me?

• See the "Answers to typical GMed interview questions" section for quick tips on how to respond to these prompts.
• Stay up-to-date on controversial medical issues and current events.
• How to prepare:

- Formulate and rehearse your answers to all common interview questions starting one week before the interview.
- Rehearse sounding non-rehearsed.

• The day before the interview, print off a few copies of your resume and do some research on the school's unique offerings.
• On interview day, be cordial: talk with other applicants about how their interviews went, talk with current students and staff during lunches and info sessions, and send out personalized "thank you" emails once the day's over.

CHAPTER 13

Making a decision

PHEW. YOU'RE DONE! Congrats! It's all over. You smell that? That's the smell of freedom. No more stupid essays to deal with, no more temperamental interviewers to suck up to, no more whiny teachers to get recs from . . . you are now a second-semester senior and you are *done-zo*. Way to go, dude.

Didn't get into any GMed programs? Don't sweat it a bit. A career in medicine is still a totally viable option for you. Not getting into a GMed program does not diminish your chances of getting into med school at all – in fact, now you'll be more prepared to ace the med school admissions process. Just work hard as an undergrad, apply to the right med schools, and you'll be all set.

Sad because you only got into 1-2 of the GMed programs you applied to, but none of your top-choice programs? Don't be. Getting into *any GMed program at all* should be your top choice, since they're all so hard to earn a seat in. It's now totally up to you to decide whether you want to go to one of the "more prestigious" undergraduate schools you got into or one of the "less prestigious" schools whose GMed program you got into. But just as a quick word in favor of the GMed programs: not having to worry about applying to med school will be a *huge* weight off your chest – trust me.

If you were accepted to all the schools/programs you wanted to get into, congrats! Catch up on all the episodes of *Saturday Night Live* you missed and go throw yourself a party or something.

As you're deciding which program to attend, there are a number of factors you'll have to carefully consider. The reasons behind everyone's decisions are different; here are some of the most common things that help people make that decision:

- Type of program (normal undergraduate program or GMed program)
- Length of GMed program (6, 7, or 8 years)
- Location
- Weather
- Size of the university
- Perceived prestige or reputation of the university or medical school
- Residency match list of its med school students
- Campus setting (urban or rural)
- Tuition and payment (i.e., can you afford this program for all 6, 7, or 8 years after factoring in aid from the FAFSA and the CSS?)
- Religious or non-denominational
- Curriculum, class sizes, and majors offered
- Atmosphere of the school
- Student life
- Residential life
- Academic and recreational facilities
- Activities and opportunities offered

You should list each of these deciding factors in order of importance and then rank each of your schools and programs based on how well they meet your criteria. Once you've made your decision, *remember to officially notify that school by May 1 that you'll be attending, and to turn down the offers of acceptance for all the other school you got into.*

Well, that's about it for now. Hope you had as much fun reading this book as I had writing it. I also hope that it helped you get the most out of your years as a high school student and out of the entire college application process. You may not fully understand the gravity of it all yet, but this is it – your future is set, you are *going* to be a doctor and you are *going* to be doing something for the rest of your life that you actually love. That's pretty big.

But don't worry, in a few years it'll all sink in and you'll really come to appreciate the program you're in. Hopefully, when that time comes, you'll look back to these years and think, wow . . . this BS/MD program – and that book – is truly more than just BS.

Summary

- You're done!!! Go crazy.
- There are a number of different factors – like prestige, tuition, and student life – that you have to consider when deciding which school or program to attend out of the ones that accepted you. Decide carefully, and then notify each school accordingly by May 1.
- . . . bye.

APPENDIX

H ERE'S A LIST of all the GMed programs in the US as of 2012. This is a good place to start when you're making a list of all the GMed programs you plan on applying to. There are tons of guaranteed medical programs out there that you can only apply to once you're in your freshman or sophomore year of college; those are excluded from this list because they aren't true "high school to med school" GMed programs.

I tried my hardest to make sure that the information in this section is as complete and up-to-date as possible, but can't *guarantee* the accuracy of any of the info here. Before you make any major decision about a school, it would be a good idea to check out their website to see if their dates or requirements have changed.

The GMed programs in this appendix are sorted alphabetically. Here's how the info on each GMed program is laid out:

Undergraduate school/university

- Affiliated Medical School
- Name of the program
- Website
- Duration of program
- MCAT required for matriculation to med school? (If so, the minimum score needed to matriculate is given here)
- Special remarks about the program

University of Alabama at Birmingham

- University of Alabama School of Medicine
- Early Medical School Acceptance Program
- http://main.uab.edu/show.asp?durki=27435
- 8 years
- MCAT? (Total: 28)
- Remarks: None.

Baylor University

- Baylor College of Medicine
- Baylor^2 Medical Track
- http://www.baylor.edu/prehealth/index.php?id=36430
- 8 years
- MCAT? No
- Remarks: Very competitive program – only 4 applicants are selected. 1 of those 4 applicants is given an $80,000 scholarship.

Boston University

- Boston University School of Medicine
- Seven-Year Liberal Arts/Medical Education Program
- http://www.bu.edu/academics/cas/programs/seven-year-liberal-arts-medical-education-program/
- 7 years
- MCAT? Yes (Total: 30)
- Remarks: None

Brooklyn College

- SUNY Downstate Medical Center College of Medicine
- BA-MD Program
- http://depthome.brooklyn.cuny.edu/bamd/bamdmain.html
- 8 years
- MCAT? Yes (Must receive 9 or above in each section. Exam can be taken up to 3 times to achieve this score.)
- Remarks: Must be a legal resident of New York, New Jersey, or Connecticut to apply. All students in the program receive a one-time $4,000 scholarship. Non-science majors are encouraged.

Brown University

- Alpert Medical School
- Program in Liberal Medical Education
- http://med.brown.edu/plme/
- 8 years
- MCAT? No
- Remarks: No on-campus GMed interview. Very focused on a broad, liberal undergraduate education.

Caldwell College

- New Jersey Medical School
- Accelerated Baccalaureate-MD Program
- http://njms.umdnj.edu/admissions/prospective/programs_7_8_year. cfm
- 7 years
- MCAT? Yes (No minimum score)
- Remarks: MCAT score is not used to determine matriculation to medical school.

California Institute of Technology

- UCSD School of Medicine
- Medical Scholars Program
- http://admissions.caltech.edu/documents/93-medscholarswithimages 2012.pdf
- 8 years
- MCAT? No
- Remarks: Emphasis on producing physician-scientists.

University of California-San Diego

- UCSD School of Medicine
- Medical Scholars Program
- http://meded.ucsd.edu/groups/med-scholars/
- 8 years
- MCAT? No
- Remarks: Must be a legal resident of California to apply.

Case Western Reserve University

- Case Western Reserve University School of Medicine
- Pre-Professional Scholars Program in Medicine
- http://admission.case.edu/apply/ppsp.aspx
- 8 years
- MCAT? No
- Remarks: Although taking the MCAT is not required, students may take it in order to apply to other medical schools or apply for a university merit scholarship. If you take the MCAT, you are expected to earn a score of at least 33.

University of Cincinnati

- University of Cincinnati College of Medicine
- Connections
- http://www.uc.edu/preproadvising/connections.html
- 8 years
- MCAT? Yes (Total: 30)
- Remarks: None.

City College of New York (Sophie Davis School of Biomedical Education)

- *Affiliated medical schools:* Albany Medical College, Dartmouth Medical School, New York Medical College, New York University School of Medicine, SUNY Health Science Center at Brooklyn, SUNY-Stony Brook School of Medicine
- BS-MD Program
- http://www1.ccny.cuny.edu/prospective/med/programs/bsmdprogram.cfm
- 7 years
- MCAT? No
- Remarks: Undergraduate curriculum is largely fixed. Must attend summer classes after 2nd and 3rd years in the program. During the fall semester of the 3rd year, you must specify which affiliated medical school you wish to attend; then, you are assigned one of those medical schools based both on your preferences and level of academic achievement. You are granted your BS degree after the 5th year of the program. Upon graduation from the program, you must be a full-time primary care physician in a primary care physician-shortage area in New York state for at least 2 years.

University of Colorado-Denver

- University of Colorado School of Medicine
- BA/BS-MD Degree Program
- http://www.ucdenver.edu/academics/colleges/CLAS/Bachelors
  Programs/ProgramsDegrees/BABSMD/Pages/home.aspx
- 8 years
- MCAT? Yes (Total: 28)
- Remarks: Must be a legal Colorado resident to apply.

University of Connecticut

- University of Connecticut School of Medicine
- Combined Program in Medicine
- http://medicine.uchc.edu/prospective/babs_md/
- 8 years
- MCAT? Yes (Total: 30)
- Remarks: There are no state residence requirements, but Connecticut applicants receive special consideration.

Drew University

- New Jersey Medical School
- Dual-Degree in Medicine
- http://www.drew.edu/undergraduate/academics/aos/
  dual-degree-in-medicine
- 7 years
- MCAT? Yes (No minimum score)
- Remarks: MCAT score is not used to determine matriculation to medical school.

Drexel University

- Drexel University College of Medicine
- BA/BS/MD Program
- http://www.drexel.edu/undergrad/apply/freshmen-instructions/
  accelerated/
- 7-8 years
- MCAT? Yes (Total: 31)
- Remarks: The program lasts 7 years for those who declare a major in biology, psychology, chemistry, or engineering, but 8 years for those who declare a major in biomedical engineering.

Duquesne University

- Temple University School of Medicine
- Duquesne Medical Scholars Program
- http://www.duq.edu/premed/professions/affiliations.cfm
- 8 years
- MCAT? Yes (Total: 30)
- Remarks: This program has 2 GMed interview dates – one at Duquesne and one at Temple School of Medicine. Temple School of Medicine makes the final admissions decision.

Florida State University

- Florida State University College of Medicine
- Honors Medical Scholars Program
- http://honors.fsu.edu/medical.html
- 7 years
- MCAT? Yes (Total: 26)
- Remarks: None.

George Washington University

- George Washington University School of Medicine and Health Sciences
- Seven-Year BA/MD Program
- http://www.gwu.edu/apply/undergraduateadmissions/learningatgw/acceleratedprograms/bamdprogram
- 7 years
- MCAT? No
- Remarks: None.

University of Hawai'i at Manoa

- University of Hawai'i at Manoa John A. Burns School of Medicine
- Doctor of Medicine Early Acceptance Program
- http://manoa.hawaii.edu/admissions/undergrad/early_admissions/
- 8 years
- MCAT? Yes (Minimum total score of 30 with no less than 9 in each section OR minimum total score of 31 with no less than 8 in each section)
- Remarks: Must be a legal resident of Hawai'i to apply. Undergraduate tuition fees are waived for students in this program.

Howard University

- Howard University College of Medicine
- BS/MD Accelerated Medical Education Program
- http://medicine.howard.edu/education/programs/degrees.htm
- 6 years
- MCAT? Yes (Total: 24)
- Remarks: None.

University of Illinois at Chicago

- University of Illinois College of Medicine
- Guaranteed Professional Program Admissions in Medicine
- http://www.uic.edu/depts/oaa/spec_prog/gppa/gppamedicine/
- 7-8 years
- MCAT? Yes (Total: 30)
- Remarks: Must be a legal resident of Illinois to apply. The program is meant to be 8 years long, but can be completed in 7 years if you finish your undergraduate studies in 3 years. If you receive an MCAT score below 30, you must take a preparatory course during the summer between undergraduate graduation and the beginning of medical school in order to keep your seat in the program.

Indiana State University

- Indiana University School of Medicine – Terre Haute
- Rural Health Program
- http://www.indstate.edu/preprof/rhp.htm
- 8 years
- MCAT? Yes (Score must be at or above the average score of the previous year's class)
- Remarks: In order to apply, you must reside in rural Indiana. All students in this program receive full tuition waivers from Indiana State University.

Indiana University-Purdue University Indianapolis

- Indiana University School of Medicine
- Honors Professional Admissions Program
- http://honorscollege.iupui.edu/hpap/
- 8 years
- MCAT? Yes (Score must be at or above the average score of the previous year's class)
- Remarks: Must be a legal resident of Indiana to apply.

Kean University

- Drexel University College of Medicine
- BS/MD Scholars Program
- http://njcste.kean.edu/programs/bsmd.html
- 8 years
- MCAT? Yes (Total: 31)
- Remarks: Emphasis on practicing general medicine in rural Pennsylvania and New Jersey.

Lehigh University

- Drexel University College of Medicine
- Combined-Degree Program in Medicine
- http://cas.lehigh.edu/casweb/default.aspx?id=129
- 7 years
- MCAT? Yes (Total: 31)
- Remarks: Undergraduates in this program must major in "Premedical Science."

University of Louisville

- University of Louisville School of Medicine
- Guaranteed Entrance to Medical School
- http://louisville.edu/admissions/aid/gep/gems
- 8 years
- MCAT? Yes (Must score at or above that year's national average for each section)
- Remarks: Must be a legal resident of Kentucky to apply.

University of Miami

- University of Miami Miller School of Medicine
- Honors Program in Medicine
- http://www.miami.edu/admission/index.php/undergraduate_admission/academics/dual_degree_honors/honors_program_in_medicine/
- 7-8 years
- MCAT? Yes (Total: 30)
- Remarks: The program can be completed in 7 years if you finish your undergraduate studies in 3 years.

Michigan Technological University

- Wayne State University School of Medicine
- MedStart
- http://www.mtu.edu/admissions/medstart/
- 8 years
- MCAT? Yes (Total: 30)
- Remarks: None.

University of Missouri-Kansas City

- UMKC School of Medicine
- Six Year BA/MD Program; or the Guaranteed Admission Baccalaureate/MD Program
- http://www.med.umkc.edu/med_admissions/BAMD.shtml
- 6-7 years
- MCAT? No
- Remarks: UMKC offers 2 separate BS/MD programs; the Guaranteed Admission Baccalaureate/MD Program is 7 years long. This program is only open to legal residents of Missouri. The curriculum for the 6 year program is largely fixed; students in this program receive a special Bachelors in Liberal Arts degree that the 7 year program students are not eligible for.

Monmouth University

- Drexel University College of Medicine
- Monmouth Medical Center Scholars Program
- http://www.monmouth.edu/academics/pre-professional_health/medical_scholars.asp

- 8 years
- MCAT? Yes (Total: 31)
- Remarks: Must be a legal resident of New Jersey to apply. Emphasis on practicing general medicine in rural Pennsylvania and New Jersey.

Montclair State University

- New Jersey Medical School
- Accelerated Baccalaureate-MD Program
- http://njms.umdnj.edu/admissions/prospective/programs 7 8 year. cfm
- 7 years
- MCAT? Yes (No minimum score)
- Remarks: MCAT score is not used to determine matriculation to medical school.

Muhlenberg College

- Drexel University College of Medicine
- Scholars-Articulation Program
- http://www.muhlenberg.edu/depts/preprof/Health Professions/ Coop Drexel.html
- 8 years
- MCAT? Yes (Must score a minimum of 9 in each section)
- Remarks: Emphasis on practicing general medicine in rural Pennsylvania and New Jersey.

University of Nevada School of Medicine

- *Affiliated undergraduate schools:* University of Nevada, Reno and University of Nevada, Las Vegas
- BS-MD Accelerated Early Admission Program
- http://www.medicine.nevada.edu/dept/asa/prospective applicants/ programs bsmd.htm
- 7 years
- MCAT? Yes (Total: 28)
- Remarks: Must be a legal resident of Nevada to apply.

The College of New Jersey

- New Jersey Medical School
- Combined BS/MD 7-year Program

- http://www.tcnj.edu/~biology/7med/med.html
- 7 years
- MCAT? Yes (No minimum score)
- Remarks: MCAT score is not used to determine matriculation to medical school.

New Jersey Institute of Technology

- New Jersey Medical School
- Accelerated Medical Program
- http://honors.njit.edu/admission/pre-health-law/
- 7 years
- MCAT? Yes (No minimum score)
- Remarks: MCAT score is not used to determine matriculation to medical school. All students admitted to this program receive a full tuition scholarship.

University of New Mexico

- University of New Mexico School of Medicine
- Combined BA/MD Degree Program
- http://hsc.unm.edu/som/combinedbamd/
- 8 years
- MCAT? Yes (Total: 26)
- Remarks: Must be a legal resident of New Mexico to apply. Emphasis on delivering health care to New Mexico's rural and underserved populations.

Northeast Ohio Medical University (NEOMED)

- *Affiliated undergraduate schools:* University of Akron, Kent State University, Youngstown State University
- BS/MD Program
- http://www.neomed.edu/admissions/medicine/bsmd
- 6-7 years
- MCAT? Yes (Total: 24)
- Remarks: Applying to NEOMED (application available at the website above) automatically makes you an applicant at all 3 affiliated undergraduate schools; each school makes its admission decision independently. Accepted students spend 2-3 years as an undergraduate at the school they were accepted to, and 4 years as a medical student at NEOMED.

Undergraduate curriculum and major are fixed. As an undergraduate, you must take classes over the summer.

Northern Michigan University

- Wayne State University School of Medicine
- MedStart
- http://www.nmu.edu/admissions/node/215
- 8 years
- MCAT? Yes (Total: 30)
- Remarks: None.

Northwestern University

- Northwestern University Feinberg School of Medicine
- Honors Program in Medical Education
- http://www.feinberg.northwestern.edu/AWOME/hpme/index.html
- 7-8 years
- MCAT? No
- Remarks: Most students choose the 7-year option; the decision is almost entirely based on personal preference.

University of Oklahoma

- University of Oklahoma College of Medicine
- Medical Humanities Scholars Program
- http://www.ou.edu/honors/MedicalHumanities/admissions.html
- 7-8 years
- MCAT? Yes (Must be at or above the average score for the previous year's class)
- Remarks: None.

Pennsylvania State University

- Jefferson Medical College
- Premedical-Medical Program
- http://science.psu.edu/premed/premedmed/accelerated-premed-medical
- 6-7 years
- MCAT? Yes (Total: 30)
- Remarks: When applying you must indicate whether you prefer the 6-year or 7-year option. In the 6-year option you receive no summers off:

undergraduate courses begin in the summer after high school graduation. In the 7-year option you receive summers off as an undergraduate. The curriculum for both options is largely predetermined. Applicants for this program are not eligible for any Penn State merit scholarships.

University of Pittsburgh

- University of Pittsburgh School of Medicine
- Guaranteed Admissions Program
- http://www.medadmissions.pitt.edu/admissions-requirements/ guaranteed-admissions.php
- 8 years
- MCAT? No
- Remarks: As an undergraduate, you must maintain a 3.75 GPA for science coursework and all coursework – this is unusually high. MCAT is not required unless you want to apply for a merit scholarship or for the school's MD/PhD program.

Rensselaer Polytechnic Institute

- Albany Medical College
- Physician-Scientist Program
- http://admissions.rpi.edu/undergraduate/academics/accelerated.html
- 7 years
- MCAT? No
- Remarks: Very research-heavy: you'll graduate Albany Medical College with an MD with Distinction in Research.

Rice University

- Baylor College of Medicine
- Rice/Baylor Medical Scholars Program
- http://futureowls.rice.edu/futureowls/Medical_Scholars.asp
- 8 years
- MCAT? No
- Remarks: Very selective program.

Richard Stockton College of New Jersey

- New Jersey Medical School
- Accelerated 7-year BS/MD Degree Program

- http://njms.umdnj.edu/admissions/prospective/programs 7 8 year. cfm
- 7 years
- MCAT? Yes (No minimum score)
- Remarks: MCAT score is not used to determine matriculation to medical school.

Robert Morris University

- Drexel University College of Medicine
- Scholars-Articulation Program
- http://www.rmu.edu/web/cms/schools/sems/science/pre-med/ Pages/drexel.aspx
- 8 years
- MCAT? Yes (Total: 31)
- Remarks: Preference is given to applicants that are legal residents of Ohio, Pennsylvania, or West Virginia and who are interested in careers in family medicine, general internal medicine, or general pediatrics. Emphasis on practicing general medicine in rural Pennsylvania and New Jersey.

University of Rochester

- University of Rochester School of Medicine and Dentistry
- Rochester Early Medical Scholars
- http://enrollment.rochester.edu/admissions/CAPs/REMS/
- 8 years
- MCAT? No
- Remarks: None.

Rosemont College

- Drexel University College of Medicine
- Early Assurance Program (8 years) and Fast Track Program (7 years)
- http://www.rosemont.edu/uc/majors/biology/rosemont-drexel-college-of-medicine-program-requirements/index.aspx
- 7-8 years
- MCAT? Yes (Total: 31)
- Remarks: Specify on your Rosemont application whether you are applying to the Early Assurance Program or the Fast Track Program. SAT/ACT requirements are slightly higher for the Fast Track Program (SAT: 1360 or ACT: 31) relative to the Early Assurance Program (SAT: 1300 or ACT: 29). Aside from that, requirements for each program are virtually the same.

Rutgers University-Newark

- New Jersey Medical School
- BA/MD Program
- http://www.ncas.rutgers.edu/office-dean-student-affairs/bamd-program-umdnj-nwk-applying
- 7 years
- MCAT? Yes (No minimum score)
- Remarks: MCAT score is not used to determine matriculation to medical school.

Siena College

- Albany Medical College
- Siena-Albany Medical College Program
- http://www.siena.edu/pages/2129.asp
- 8 years
- MCAT? No
- Remarks: Undergraduates in this program must major in biology and minor in a subject in the humanities.

St. Bonaventure University

- George Washington University School of Medicine and Health Sciences
- Dual Admissions Program
- http://www.sbu.edu/about_sbu.aspx?id=6230
- 8 years
- MCAT? No
- Remarks: This program emphasizes community service – as an undergraduate you must complete a summer internship in community service at a rural or urban health facility.

St. Peter's University

- Drexel University College of Medicine
- Joint BA/MD Program
- http://www.spc.edu/pages/4041.asp
- 8 years
- MCAT? Yes (Total: 31)
- Remarks: None.

St. Peter's University

- New Jersey Medical School
- Articulated Program
- http://njms.umdnj.edu/admissions/prospective/programs_articulated.cfm
- 7 years
- MCAT? Yes (A "good MCAT score" is needed to matriculate)
- Remarks: None.

Stevens Institute of Technology

- New Jersey Medical School
- Accelerated Pre-Medicine Program
- http://www.stevens.edu/sit/admissions/academics/preprofessional.cfm
- 7 years
- MCAT? Yes (No minimum score)
- Remarks: MCAT score is not used to determine matriculation to medical school. Undergraduate curriculum is largely fixed: students must major in chemical biology and are expected to conduct 2 summers of scientific research.

Stony Brook University

- Stony Brook School of Medicine
- Scholars for Medicine
- http://www.stonybrook.edu/ugadmissions/newhonors/scholarsmed.shtml
- 8 years
- MCAT? Yes (Total score must be at or above the national average for that year)
- Remarks: None.

SUNY Upstate Medical University

- *Affiliated undergraduate schools:* Clarkson University, Hobart and William Smith Colleges, St. Bonaventure University, St. Lawrence University, Sienna College, SUNY-Geneseo, SUNY-ESF, SUNY-Potsdam, Wilkes University
- Each undergraduate school has a different name for this program
- http://www.upstate.edu/com/admissions/options/
- 8 years
- MCAT? Yes (Total: 30)

• Remarks: Must be a rural New York state resident to apply. Emphasis on rural medicine. If admitted, you will be enrolled in the Rural Medical Scholars Program as a medical student, which involves taking special classes and clinical electives in rural medicine.

Texas A&M Health Sciences Center College of Medicine

• *Affiliated undergraduate schools:* Prairie View A&M University, South Texas College, Tarleton State University, Texas A&M International University, Texas A&M University, West Texas A&M University
• Partnership for Primary Care
• http://medicine.tamhsc.edu/admissions/ppc/index.html
• 8 years
• MCAT? Yes (Total: 25)
• Remarks: Must be a legal resident of a rural, underserved, or physician-shortage area of Texas to apply, as defined by the Texas Department of Health. This program heavily emphasizes providing primary care to underserved areas of Texas.

University of Texas Medical Branch-Galveston

• *Affiliated undergraduate schools:* Prairie View A&M University, Texas A&M International University, Texas Southern University, University of Texas-Brownsville, University of Texas-El Paso, University of Texas-Pan American
• Early Medical School Acceptance Program
• http://www.utmb.edu/somstudentaffairs/specialprograms/acceptance program.html
• 8 years
• MCAT? Yes (Total: 24)
• Remarks: Must be a legal resident of Texas to apply. Undergraduate students in this program must major in biology or chemistry.

University of Texas-Pan American

• Baylor College of Medicine
• Premedical Honors College Program
• http://portal.utpa.edu/utpa_main/daa_home/cose_home/biology_home/biology_jp/jp_pmh
• 8 years
• MCAT? Yes (Total: 28)

- Remarks: Must be a resident of south Texas to apply. Undergraduates in this program must major in biology, chemistry, or biochemistry.

Texas Tech University

- Texas Tech University Health Sciences Center School of Medicine
- Undergraduate to Medical School Initiative
- http://www.ttuhsc.edu/som/admissions/umsi.aspx
- 8 years
- MCAT? No
- Remarks: Must be a legal resident of Texas to apply.

University of Toledo

- University of Toledo College of Medicine
- There are 2 GMed programs at this school: the Baccalaureate/MD Program and the BS/MD Program
- *Baccalaureate/MD Program:* http://www.utoledo.edu/offices/student services/preprofessional/Baccalaureate_MD_Program.html *BS/MD Program:* http://www.bioe.eng.utoledo.edu/undergraduate/programs/ bsmd.html
- *Baccalaureate/MD:* 7 years; *BS/MD:* 8-9 years
- *Baccalaureate/MD:* MCAT? No; *BS/MD:* MCAT? No
- Remarks: Applicants cannot apply to both programs – they can choose only one. The Baccalaureate/MD gives preference to applicants that are Ohio residents. BS/MD undergraduate students must hold internship positions in research labs and/or the biomedical industry. The length and number of these internships determine whether the program lasts for 8 or 9 years.

Union College

- Albany Medical College
- Leadership in Medicine
- http://www.union.edu/offices/lim/
- 8 years
- MCAT? No
- Remarks: Applications initially reviewed by Union then forwarded to Albany if qualified. During the first 4 years of the program, you'll earn not only a BS, but also either an MS or an MBA.

Ursinus College

- Drexel University College of Medicine
- Medical School Early Assurance Program
- http://www.ursinus.edu/NetCommunity/Page.aspx?pid=440& srcid=193
- 8 years
- MCAT? Yes (Total: 31)
- Remarks: None.

Villanova University

- Drexel University College of Medicine
- Medical Affiliate Program
- http://www1.villanova.edu/villanova/artsci/undergrad/health/ affiliates/medicine.html
- 7 years
- MCAT? Yes (Total: 31)
- Remarks: Although you're allowed to major in anything you want, a major in the biological sciences is highly recommended.

Virginia Commonwealth University

- VCU School of Medicine
- Guaranteed Admission Program in Medicine
- https://www.pubapps.vcu.edu/honors/guaranteed/medicine/
- 8 years
- MCAT? No
- Remarks: None.

Washington & Jefferson College

- Temple University School of Medicine
- Washington & Jefferson Medical Scholars Program
- http://www.washjeff.edu/pre-health-program/health-professions- school-affliations
- 8 years
- MCAT? Yes (Each section: must score at or above the 70th percentile for that year)
- Remarks: This program has 2 GMed interview dates – one at Washington & Jefferson and one at Temple School of Medicine. Temple School of Medicine makes the final admissions decision.

Washington University in St. Louis

- Washington University School of Medicine in St. Louis
- University Scholars Program in Medicine
- http://admissions.wustl.edu/faq/Pages/USP.aspx
- 8 years
- MCAT? Yes (Total: 36)
- Remarks: Academic standards for this program are very high: undergraduate students in the program must maintain a 3.8 GPA to matriculate.

Wayne State University

- Wayne State University School of Medicine
- MedStart
- http://www.honors.wayne.edu/medstart.php
- 8 years
- MCAT? Yes (Total: 30)
- Remarks: All students in the program are given a Presidential Scholarship valued at $40,000.

West Chester University

- Drexel University College of Medicine
- Early Assurance Program
- http://www.wcupa.edu/_ACADEMICS/SCH_CAS/MED/Early_Assurance_Undergrad/drexel.asp
- 8 years
- MCAT? Yes (Total: 31)
- Remarks: None.

Widener University

- Temple University School of Medicine
- Widener Medical Scholars Program
- http://www.widener.edu/academics/collegesandschools/artsand sciences/sciences/premedicalstudies/medscholars.asp
- 8 years
- MCAT? Yes (Minimum score not specified)
- Remarks: Must be a legal resident of Pennsylvania, Delaware, New Jersey, or Maryland to apply. This program has 2 GMed interview dates – one at Widener and one at Temple School of Medicine. Temple School of

Medicine makes the final admissions decision. Strong emphasis placed on primary care: general pediatrics, internal medicine, and family medicine in particular.

Wilkes University

- Pennsylvania State University College of Medicine at Hershey
- Premedical Scholars Program
- http://bulletin.wilkes.edu/7429.htm
- 8 years
- MCAT? Yes (Score in each section must be at or above the average score of the previous year's class)
- Remarks: "Emphasis in recruiting will be placed on students from rural and/or medically underserved areas of Pennsylvania who wish to pursue a career in primary care medicine."

ABOUT THE AUTHOR

JAYSON MARWAHA IS a student in Brown University's Program in Liberal Medical Education – an 8-year combined BS/MD program. Given his natural disposition as a worrywart (he refuses to stop worrying about the ending of *Inception* until *Inception 2* comes out to clear things up), he made a point to apply only to guaranteed medical programs. With his time in college he has managed to:

- Found and run an NGO (and haughtily introduce himself as a daring "entrepreneur" at parties),
- Write a book,
- Study abroad,
- Take weird classes,
- Quickly pack well beyond a Freshman 15,
- And just have a great time in college.

With his free time on Sunday mornings, in the cafeteria over a plate of gelatinous scrambled eggs, Jayson loves to read. His favorite work of fine American literature, you ask? . . . well, this one.

Made in the USA
Lexington, KY
28 October 2016